THE CALL TO FOLLOW CHRIST

CLAUDE KING

with a music CD by Dámaris Carbaugh

LifeWay Press®
Nashville, Tennessee

ISBN 978-1-4158-3262-2
Item 001303666

Dewey decimal classification: 248.84
Subject heading: DISCIPLESHIP \ CHRISTIAN LIFE

Cover illustration: Mac Premo

Unless otherwise noted, all Scripture quotations are taken from
the Holman Christian Standard Bible®, copyright © 1999, 2000, 2001, 2002, 2003
by Holman Bible Publishers. Used by permission.

Scripture quotations marked KJV are from the King James Version of the Bible.

Scriptures marked NKJV are from the New King James Version. Copyright © 1979, 1980, 1982,
Thomas Nelson, Inc. Publishers.

Scriptures marked NIV are from the Holy Bible, New International Version,
copyright © 1973, 1978, 1984 by International Bible Society.

To order additional copies of this resource: write to
LifeWay Church Resources Customer Service; One LifeWay Plaza; Nashville, TN 37234-0113;
fax (615) 251-5933; phone toll free (800) 458-2772; order online at *www.lifeway.com;* e-mail
orderentry@lifeway.com; or visit the LifeWay Christian Store serving you.

Printed in the United States of America

Leadership and Adult Publishing
LifeWay Church Resources
One LifeWay Plaza
Nashville, TN 37234-0175

Contents

Introducing
Claude King and Dámaris Carbaugh

Claude King is an editor in chief for leadership and adult undated resources at LifeWay Christian Resources. In 1990 he coauthored *Experiencing God: Knowing and Doing the Will of God* with Henry Blackaby, which has sold over 5 million copies and has been translated into over 50 languages. He has written or coauthored over 20 other books and discipleship resources. Claude serves on the board of directors for Final Command Ministries. He is a graduate of Belmont College and New Orleans Baptist Theological Seminary. He is married to Reta and has two daughters and one grandson. Other LifeWay courses written or coauthored by Claude King include: *Fresh Encounter* with Henry Blackaby, *The Mind of Christ* with T. W. Hunt, and *Come to the Lord's Table.*

Dámaris Carbaugh has known the heights of success in the New York City recording community. She's sung in commercial jingles for some of the world's biggest advertisers, including Coca-Cola, Pepsi, Kentucky Fried Chicken, Minute Maid, and Wrigley's Doublemint Gum. Yet the desire of her heart is to be a servant of Christ. "I don't want a career," she says, "I want to be faithful." Dámaris has frequently been a soloist with the Brooklyn Tabernacle Choir in New York City, and she is also a soloist and member of the Discovery Singers for the "Day of Discovery" television program produced by Radio Bible Class. She has recorded numerous solo music CDs, including *The Call,* from which we have drawn seven songs to share with you throughout this course. Dámaris and her husband, Rod, have two adult children. You can find out more about her ministry, music, and concert schedule at her Web site, *www.damariscarbaugh.com.*

Let's Follow Christ Together

Hello! I'm Claude, and I have the privilege of spending the next seven weeks with you as we seek to follow Jesus Christ more faithfully. I am a bit overwhelmed at this assignment. Who am I to teach you how to follow Christ? That's a huge responsibility. Yet I am comforted to know that I'm not alone in this task.

God gave us His Word to teach and guide us—what a gift! And He's placed His Holy Spirit in His children (you and me) to be our Teacher and to help us apply the truths of His Word to our lives. (I'm making the assumption that you have placed your faith in Jesus Christ and that you have a personal relationship with Him. If that is not the case, talk to a pastor or a Christian friend about how you can enter that relationship before we get started.) The Holy Spirit is going to point us to Christ and help us to know Him and experience Him at work in us and through us. Jesus once said to some religious leaders, "You pore over the Scriptures because you think you have eternal life in them, yet they testify about Me. And you are not willing to come to Me that you may have life" (John 5:39-40). Here's the plan: I want us to study the Scriptures together. Then we'll take one more step to a relationship with Jesus Christ in which He will guide us to experience the abundant life He came to give us.

SMALL-GROUP STUDY OF *THE CALL TO FOLLOW CHRIST*

But let's not stop there. Although you could study this book alone, I want you to experience God's best. When God saved you, He placed you in the body of Christ so that you can benefit from the ministry of the other members of the body. You are also in the body to contribute to helping others. The writer of Hebrews instructs us: "Let us consider how we may spur one another on toward love and good deeds. Let us not give up meeting together, as some are in the habit of doing, but let us encourage one another" (Hebrews 10:24-25). Will you do that with me? Join a group of other believers in Christ. If necessary, enlist some to join you in your study so that you can help one another grow in following Christ. You will find that we need one another, and we can help one another. Let's do it.

If you are the person who will lead the small-group sessions, I've included a brief leader guide beginning on page 101. For each of the seven sessions I've included suggested learning activities to guide your sharing, processing, and applying the things you are learning. If you are not the group leader, you may still want to look at the session plans on pages 104–10 so that you will be prepared to respond to the things your leader guides you to do. Before the study ends, you will experience a special closeness to your small group. You will experience some of the benefits God intended when He created the church as the body of Christ.

MESSAGE MUSIC

I've also got some help from a dear friend, Dámaris Carbaugh. In 2003 while working in New York City, I attended a prayer breakfast at the United Nations as the General

Assembly prepared to open. Dámaris sang that day, and I had the privilege of meeting her and her husband, Rod. I had been deeply impacted by her music for years. Two of her songs had particularly touched me: "Willingly" and "Whatever It Takes." In fact, God had used those songs to prepare me to answer His call to serve in New York City. She and Rod invited me to visit their church on Sunday for an outdoor concert.

After the service they took me to dinner, and I heard about *The Call* (see p. 112). Dámaris and 80 people in her church had been studying *MasterLife,* a discipleship course by Avery T. Willis Jr. When her music publisher asked her to select a theme for her next recording project, she suggested that the writers use *MasterLife* as the source of their work. A few weeks later, 10 songs were ready for recording. That night at dinner she began to sing for me some of the songs she had just recorded. Wow! I was moved.

Two years later, I returned to work at LifeWay, the publisher of *MasterLife.* I made a proposal for *The Call to Follow Christ,* based on six disciplines taught in *MasterLife.* I'm thrilled that Discovery House Music has permitted us to use seven songs from *The Call* to enrich your study and to develop the six disciplines in your life. I call these songs message music. The songs have a powerful message that can help us grow in our walk with Christ and development of these spiritual disciplines. Each week I'll introduce you to one of the songs and guide you to interact with the message in the music. But you don't have to wait to listen to all seven songs. Go ahead and let God begin using these messages to saturate your heart and mind with the desire to answer His call to follow Christ.

PERSONAL STUDY OF *THE CALL TO FOLLOW CHRIST*
This book may be different from others you have read. I call this a self-paced, interactive study. I'm not just speaking to you as I write. I want you to interact with me and with the Lord. So I will give you instructions for at least two types of activities.

 One is a prayer activity that begins with an arrow pointing up to God and down to you. The arrow symbolizes what I want you to do in prayer. Talk to the Lord and listen as He speaks to you. At the beginning of each day I will ask you to listen to God through His Word; you'll read a verse or two from the Bible. Then I'll ask you to meditate and pray. At other times I will give you suggestions for a time of prayer. While we're here, take a moment to pray and ask God to guide you and speak to you as you pray to Him over the next seven weeks.

① The other kind of activity will begin with a circled number. In these learning activities I may ask you a question and give you instructions for responding. Or I may give you instructions about something I want you to do. Take these learning activities seriously. Don't just skip over them to move on in your reading. I don't want you just to read some information about following Christ. I want you to understand the message, and I want you to apply it to your life. These learning activities will help you understand and apply these truths to your life. Will you work with me by completing these learning activities? Check your response: ○ yes ○ no

I hope you answered yes. If you answered no, you'll miss much of the help this study can provide for your spiritual growth. After the learning activities I may give you some feedback about your response as I'm doing now. If there are correct answers, I will provide them either in the following paragraph or in the margin.

Each week you will study five daily lessons before getting together with a mentor or a small group to process what you are leaning. Don't wait until the end of the week to start your study. I don't want you to be overwhelmed by having too much to do in too short a time. That can be discouraging. But more importantly, I want you to develop a habit of spending time with God every day. Some people call this a quiet time or devotional time. Take some time every day (preferably at the beginning of the day) to read God's Word, study or meditate on its meaning, and talk to God in prayer. For the next seven weeks, let this book be your guide. By starting the day with your focus on Christ, you will be in a position all day to let God apply the truths to your life. As you do this in "chewable bites" (or small pieces at a time), you will learn and grow at a reasonable pace. You will need to study week 1 before your first small-group session.

I will also ask you to memorize some Bible verses. These Scriptures can guide you, encourage you, warn you, or give you a promise from God to keep in your mind. I've chosen a verse for each week that will apply to the discipline for the week. One of your lessons in week 3 will help you understand better why memorizing Scripture is valuable. Just take my word for it: this will be worth your effort! The first week's study provides tips for memorizing Scripture.

THE DISCIPLE'S CROSS

For years I worked with Avery T. Willis Jr., who had written the discipleship course called *MasterLife*. Probably half a million people or more have studied this course just as the people at Dámaris Carbaugh's church did. It is being used all around the world. *The Call to Follow Christ* is an introduction to the six disciplines taught in *MasterLife*. After you finish this study, you may want to move into the four courses in *MasterLife* to grow much deeper and stronger in your walk with Christ.

In *MasterLife* Avery organizes the six disciplines into what I call a course "map." His "map" is called the Disciple's Cross. I'll introduce it to you in week 2, but you can take a peek now on page 93. As you study the diagram, you will see all six disciplines on or around the cross. This can be a valuable memory aid for your own discipleship journey. I will use it for that purpose. However, it can also be a valuable tool for you to teach others what a life of following Christ looks like. With that purpose in mind, your small-group leader or mentor will probably ask you to describe parts of the diagram week by week. Watch for opportunities to draw and describe the Disciple's Cross. That will help you learn the disciplines and may help you bring another person to our Savior, Jesus Christ.

Well, the time has come. Let's get started on our journey of following Jesus!

GROWING DISCIPLES SERIES

THE CALL TO
FOLLOW CHRIST

Six Disciplines for New
and Growing Believers

Claude King

Week 1 • Introducing *The Call to Follow Christ*

"If anyone wants to come with Me, he must
deny himself, take up his cross daily, and
follow Me" (Luke 9:23).

Introducing *The Call to Follow Christ*

God has chosen and called believers into a real love relationship with Jesus Christ that is joyful, meaningful, and fruitful. Following Christ requires denying self, taking up our cross daily, and following Him in obedience. Following Christ is reflected through a disciplined life in our relationship with Him, other believers, and the rest of the world.

OVERVIEW OF WEEK 1

Day 1: Chosen by Christ and Called
Day 2: Called to Follow
Day 3: Three Requirements for Following
Day 4: Christ-Centered Following
Day 5: Introducing Six Disciplines

VERSE TO MEMORIZE

"If anyone wants to come with Me, he must deny himself, take up his cross daily, and follow Me" (Luke 9:23).

MESSAGE-MUSIC CD

"The Call" (track 1)

DISCIPLESHIP HELPS FOR WEEK 1

"Tips for Memorizing Scripture" (p. 92)

WHY THIS WEEK WILL BE MEANINGFUL TO YOU

You will understand God's calling on your life to follow Christ. You will show your willingness to follow Christ by doing such things as …

- praying a prayer of surrender to Him and His will;
- describing to Him your desire to be a faithful follower;
- choosing to deny self so that you can freely follow His will;
- taking up your cross daily, which puts sin to death in your life;
- studying Scriptures diligently and moving through them into a relationship with Christ to understand and live by the spirit of His Word;
- developing spiritual disciplines in your life that strengthen Christlikeness, demonstrate obedience, and yield spiritual fruitfulness.

Day 1 • Chosen by Christ and Called

Read and briefly meditate on "God's Word for Today" in the margin and respond to the Lord in prayer. As your time permits, consider the "Optional Reading" each day. Read it in your Bible and mark verses that are meaningful or that you would like to memorize. As you read, pause and talk to God about what you are reading. Cultivate your relationship with Him.

The night before Jesus laid down His life on the cross, He spoke to His followers. These instructions are also for us as followers of Christ. Here's one:

> I have spoken these things to you so that My joy may be in you and your joy may be complete. This is My command: love one another as I have loved you. No one has greater love than this, that someone would lay down his life for his friends. You are My friends if you do what I command you. I do not call you slaves anymore, because a slave doesn't know what his master is doing. I have called you friends, because I have made known to you everything I have heard from My Father. You did not choose Me, but I chose you. I appointed you that you should go out and produce fruit and that your fruit should remain (John 15:11-16).

1. **Which statement would you choose as the most meaningful to you? Check one or underline a phrase from John 15:11-16 above.**
   - ○ a. He wants my joy to be complete.
   - ○ b. He showed His great love for me when He laid down His life for me.
   - ○ c. I don't have to be a slave of God; I can be His friend.
   - ○ d. Out of all people on earth, He chose me and gave me an assignment.
   - ○ e. His plan is to produce spiritual fruit through my life that will last.

As we begin our study together, we have every reason to be amazed. Jesus, the Savior and Creator, has chosen us to be His friends and coworkers. He has planned that we will be fruitful—spiritually successful. He has every intention to fill us with His joy, and best of all, He loved us so deeply that He went to the cross and gave His life for us. What a privilege to follow such a Savior. In addition to being chosen, we are also called.*

2. **Read 1 Peter 2:9 in the margin on the next page and circle the word *called*.**

   What are you called from? _____ And to?_____

God's Word for Today
"His divine power has given us everything we need for life and godliness through our knowledge of him who called us by his own glory and goodness."
2 Peter 1:3, NIV

Responding to the Lord
Wow! Lord, I didn't know when I first came to You that Your divine power would give me everything I need for life and godliness. In fact, I don't think I've fully experienced the truth of that promise. But I sure want to. Lord, You are good and glorious. You have called me. I've joined this study because I want to follow You, but I need Your help. Empower me to live the life You have called me to live. I ask this in Jesus' name and according to Your promise. Amen.

Optional Reading
2 Peter 1

Called: invited, summoned by God to partake of the blessings of salvation and redemption

🎧 As you read the words below, listen to Dámaris sing "The Call" (track 1) on the message-music CD. In the chorus underline the other things to which you are called. I've underlined one for you.

It's a stirring in my spirit / It's a tugging at my heart
It's the voice of everlasting / Speaking in my deepest part
And as I read the Scripture / It leaps off of the page
It leads me as I worship / And draws me when I pray

Chorus
It's the call <u>to trust</u> / The call to love / The call to walk by faith
The call to go / And the call to serve / To follow and obey
He is worthy indeed / Oh, will you heed the call

The question lies before us / A decision we must make
Oh, will we follow Jesus / Or hold to our own way
We must not take it lightly / 'Cause it touches everything
It's a lifelong surrender / To heaven's gracious King
    Repeat chorus
The call is like a whisper / The call is like a shout
And it's the invitation / True life is all about
    Repeat chorus

③ The call of Jesus is to a "lifelong surrender / To heaven's gracious King." "Will you heed the call"? Check your answer below.
  ○ a. I choose to follow Jesus—to trust, to love, to walk by faith, to go, to serve, to follow and obey.
  ○ b. I'm sorry, but I'm still going to hold to my own way.

I pray that your answer is *a*. It's a huge choice, isn't it? If you are still at answer *b*, stick with us. Paul wrote, "It is God who is working in you, enabling you both to will and to act for His good purpose" (Philippians 2:13). God hasn't called you to do or be anything that He will not also enable you to be or do in order to fulfill His purpose. He will even help you want to do His will.

 Ask the Lord to make clear to you His calling on your life. Tell Him about your willingness to surrender to His will as He makes it clear to you. Ask the Lord to help you respond to His call in faith, obedience, and full surrender. If you're not ready to pray like this, would you at least give Him permission to help you want to follow His call? If so, do it.

The Call

1 Peter 2:9
"You are 'a chosen race,
    a royal priesthood,
a holy nation, a people
    for His possession,
so that you may proclaim
    the praises'
of the One who called
    you out of darkness
into His marvelous light."

God hasn't called you to do or be anything that He will not also enable you to be or do in order to fulfill His purpose.

Day 2 • Called to Follow

 Read and briefly meditate on "God's Word for Today" in the margin and respond to the Lord in prayer.

God has called us into a relationship with Jesus Christ, the Good Shepherd (John 10:11). As sheep, we will know His voice and follow Him (John 10:27-28).

① **Read the Scriptures under "Called" in the margin on pages 12–13, and underline the words *called* and *calling* each time they occur. I've underlined one for you. In each verse, notice that to which you've been called.**

My brother or sister in Christ, God has called us to salvation, to eternal life, to hope, to be saints, to an eternal inheritance and eternal glory. We've been called out of darkness and into His marvelous light!

JESUS CALLED DISCIPLES TO FOLLOW HIM

When Jesus began His earthly ministry, He called 12 men to follow Him and learn from Him. He called them to be with Him so that they could learn from His words as well as His example and lifestyle. He called these men to train and equip them to carry on His mission after He returned to heaven.

② **As you read about Jesus' calling of some of these men, underline the words that describe how they responded to His call. What did they do?**

Simon Peter and Andrew. "As He was walking along the Sea of Galilee, He saw two brothers, Simon, who was called Peter, and his brother Andrew. They were casting a net into the sea, since they were fishermen. 'Follow Me,' He told them, 'and I will make you fish for people!' Immediately they left their nets and followed Him" (Matthew 4:18-20).

James and John. "Going on from there, He saw two other brothers, James the son of Zebedee, and his brother John. They were in a boat with Zebedee their father, mending their nets, and He called them. Immediately they left the boat and their father and followed Him" (Matthew 4:21-22).

Levi (Matthew). "After this, Jesus went out and saw a tax collector named Levi sitting at the tax office, and He said to him, 'Follow Me!' So, leaving everything behind, he got up and began to follow Him" (Luke 5:27-28).

God's Word for Today

"My sheep hear My voice, I know them, and they follow Me. I give them eternal life, and they will never perish— ever! No one will snatch them out of My hand."
John 10:27-28

Responding to the Lord

Lord Jesus, thank You for calling me and making me one of Your sheep. What a gift You have given me—eternal life and security in Your hand! Help me know Your voice so that I may follow You faithfully. Amen.

Optional Reading

1 Peter 2

John 10:11

"I am the good shepherd. The good shepherd lays down his life for the sheep."

Called

• "To all who are … loved by God, <u>called</u> as saints" (Romans 1:7).

• "All things work together for the good of those who love God: those who are called according to His purpose" (Romans 8:28).

These five, plus seven more, chose to follow Christ when He called them. Simon Peter and Andrew *immediately* left their fishing nets and followed. James and John also *immediately* left their family fishing business and their father to follow Christ. Levi left everything behind, including his tax-collecting career, to follow Christ. For three years they followed Him, and He readied them to carry on His work. He prepared them to carry out one great assignment that He would give them at the end of their training: "Go, therefore, and make disciples of all nations" (Matthew 28:19). By the time Jesus returned to heaven, at least 120 people had believed and chosen to follow Him (see Acts 1:15).

CALLED TO BE A DISCIPLE

A disciple* is a learner, one who follows the teachings of another. A disciple is one who becomes like his master or teacher, one who imitates his teacher. When you answer the call to follow Christ, you begin the process of becoming a disciple, too. He is your Lord and Master. He wants you to follow Him.

(3) **Read the definition of *disciple* in the right margin below. Which of the following is the best definition of a disciple of Christ? Check one.**
- O a. A person who reads about Jesus and can answer questions about His life and teachings
- O b. A person who learns about Christ and His teachings and chooses to live like Him and to obey His commands
- O c. A person who chooses to live the way he or she desires without any reference to what Christ wants

Did you choose answer *b?* That's correct. A person who chooses not to follow Christ's commands *(c)* is not a disciple. Neither is a person who only knows about Christ and His teachings. A disciple is one who follows. Jesus has called you to be on mission with Him. As your Lord, He has chosen and called you to be His servant and follower. Jesus said, "If anyone serves Me, he must follow Me. Where I am, there My servant also will be. If anyone serves Me, the Father will honor him" (John 12:26).

(4) **If Jesus Christ evaluated the quality of your following Him, what grade do you think He would give? Check one.**
- O a. A—excellent follower
- O c. I—improving
- O b. B—very good follower
- O d. N—needs improvement

Thank Jesus for calling you to His salvation and eternal life. Talk to Jesus about your desire to be His faithful follower.

- "I pray that the eyes of your heart may be enlightened so you may know what is the hope of His calling" (Ephesians 1:18).
- "There is one body and one Spirit, just as you were called to one hope at your calling" (Ephesians 4:4).
- "Take hold of eternal life, to which you were called" (1 Timothy 6:12).
- "He is the mediator of a new covenant, so that those who are called might receive the promise of the eternal inheritance" (Hebrews 9:15).
- "You are 'a chosen race, a royal priesthood, a holy nation, a people for His possession, so that you may proclaim the praises' of the One who called you out of darkness into His marvelous light" (1 Peter 2:9).
- "The God of all grace, who called you to His eternal glory in Christ Jesus, will personally restore, establish, strengthen, and support you" (1 Peter 5:10).

Disciple: a learner, one who follows the teachings of another, an adherent, an imitator of the teacher

Day 3 • Three Requirements for Following

↕ **Read and briefly meditate on "God's Word for Today" in the margin and respond to the Lord in prayer. Use the written prayer or pray your own.**

Following Jesus is costly. Not everyone who met Him chose to follow Him. Many turned away. Not all those He called were willing to pay the price to follow Him. Jesus described this journey of following Him as a narrow way and a difficult road that few find. He's not hiding the cost; He invites you to it. But you have to choose to follow. I'm glad that you are indicating your desire to follow by studying this book with me. The benefits are well worth the cost!

Let's briefly look at what Jesus asks of His followers in Luke 9:23-24. Jesus mentions three things you must do to follow Him.

① **Read Luke 9:23-24 ("God's Word for Today") and fill in the blanks below.**

"If anyone wants to come with Me, he must _____ himself,

take up his _____ daily, and _____ Me."

DENY SELF
Self-centeredness is at the heart of our sinful nature. Pride demands its rights and wants its own way. The pride that lives is us has the idea that we know better how to live our lives than our Creator does. We want to live our own way. When Jesus calls us to be His followers, He calls us to repent (Matthew 4:17). To repent*, we turn away from living life our way, and we choose to make Him Lord. We decide to live life His way, according to His will.

② **What is the first thing Jesus asks you to do to follow Him?**

_____

TAKE UP YOUR CROSS DAILY
Jesus died on a cross to pay the penalty for your sin. His payment was sufficient for all your sin. He purchased the forgiveness He freely offers to you, but Jesus also died to win victory over sin. Because of Christ, you do not have to live under sin's control any longer. Though a follower of Christ may sin, he doesn't have to sin. Paul described his experience this way: "I have been crucified with

---

God's Word for Today
"[Jesus] said to them all, 'If anyone wants to come with Me, he must deny himself, take up his cross daily, and follow Me. For whoever wants to save his life will lose it, but whoever loses his life because of Me will save it.'"
Luke 9:23-24

Responding to the Lord
Jesus, I want to follow You. That's why I'm doing this study. But it sounds costly. I'm not sure I'm up to the task. I know, though, that You are the One who will work in me to cause me to want to do Your will and then help me do it. Please help me. Teach me what You mean by denying myself, taking up my cross daily, and following You. I want to follow You. Amen.

Optional Reading
Luke 5:1-32

✳ *Repent:* to change one's mind, to turn from sin and to God

Matthew 4:17
"Jesus began to preach, 'Repent, because the kingdom of heaven has come near!'"

Christ; and I no longer live, but Christ lives in me" (Galatians 2:19-20). You can die to self and to sin because the Spirit of Christ living in you is able to help you live free from sin. This may seem like an impossible dream, but it can be your everyday reality. You take up your cross daily by dying to self and sin.

③ Read the selected verses from Romans 6 in the margin. Then write a statement describing the truth about the influence of sin in your life.

_____

_____

The truth about your relationship to sin is this: you are dead to sin. Sin's dominion over you is abolished. You are no longer enslaved to sin, and it no longer rules over you. You are, however, enslaved to God's righteousness. Sin is a choice you make. When you choose to obey your sinful nature, you are enslaved to sin. But you can choose to obey and follow Christ! That's the truth! You are now a slave to righteousness.

Many followers of Christ are not experiencing this truth God has made possible. But Christ has set us free from bondage to sin. My prayer is that during this study you will increasingly experience this reality. Don't give up by thinking the standard is too high. We'll learn this truth together: what is impossible for us is possible with God. Today (and daily) choose to obey Christ and die on your cross to sin. Victory is won moment by moment, then hour by hour, and God can enable you to experience the reality of Romans 6 all day today!

④ Denying self is the first requirement. What is the second requirement for one who wants to follow Christ?

_____

FOLLOW ME

When you choose to deny yourself, you turn from living life your way to living life Christ's way. You choose to put to death your sinful nature and decide to obey Christ and His righteousness. Now you follow Him. All three requirements go together. You choose to make Him your Master and Lord. You obey Him. You live like Him. By His Spirit you think and act like Him.

 God welcomes your honesty in prayer. Tell Him what you are thinking. Then in faith ask Him to empower you to follow Christ. He will!

Romans 6:6-7,11

"We know that our old self was crucified with Him in order that sin's dominion over the body may be abolished, so that we may no longer be enslaved to sin, since a person who has died is freed from sin's claims. So, you too consider yourselves dead to sin, but alive to God in Christ Jesus."

Romans 6:12,14

"Do not let sin reign in your mortal body, so that you obey its desires. For sin will not rule over you."

Romans 6:16-18,22

"Do you not know that if you offer yourselves to someone as obedient slaves, you are slaves of that one you obey—either of sin leading to death or of obedience leading to righteousness? But thank God that, although you used to be slaves of sin, you obeyed from the heart that pattern of teaching you were entrusted to, and having been liberated from sin, you became enslaved to righteousness. But now, since you have been liberated from sin and become enslaved to God, you have your fruit, which results in sanctification—and the end is eternal life!"

Day 4 • Christ-Centered Following

 Read and briefly meditate on "God's Word for Today" in the margin and respond to the Lord in prayer. Use the written prayer or pray your own.

God's Word for Today
"You pore over the Scriptures because you think you have eternal life in them, yet they testify about Me. And you are not willing to come to Me that you may have life."
John 5:39–40

Responding to the Lord
Lord Jesus, that doesn't sound good. I don't want that to be said about my life. I want to experience all of life that You have for me. I am willing to come to You. Show me how. Amen.

Optional Reading
John 5

Mark 12:24
"Are you not deceived because you don't know the Scriptures or the power of God?"

Jesus' first disciples had one privilege over followers today. Jesus was physically present for them to talk to, learn from, and follow. Now that Jesus is in heaven, He has given us His Holy Spirit to live in us and guide us. His Holy Spirit is always present to guide us to understand and follow Him.

In Jesus' day, people followed God in ways that were not adequate. We can see similar approaches to following Christ today. I see three approaches to knowing, understanding, and applying God's Word in following Him.

THE HUMAN-CENTERED APPROACH:
THE WAY OF THE SADDUCEES
The Sadducees or "righteous ones" were religious leaders in Jesus' day. They did not believe in resurrection, but they came to Jesus with a question about the resurrection. Jesus responded by saying, "Are you not deceived because you don't know the Scriptures or the power of God?" (Mark 12:24). They used their human reasoning and personal experience to determine whether their beliefs were right or wrong. Their error was that their beliefs were not in line with the Scriptures because they were not sufficiently familiar with them. The Sadducees were also in error because they did not have an experiential knowledge of God's power. Many people today try to use their own reasoning to determine right from wrong or to know God's will. Such people are greatly deceived.

(1) What were the errors of the Sadducees identified in Mark 12:24?

They did not know the _____ or the _____ of God.

THE SCRIPTURE-CENTERED APPROACH:
THE WAY OF THE JEWS (PHARISEES)
Another group of Jewish leaders, probably the Pharisees, used a different approach to knowing, understanding, and applying God's Word. They condemned Jesus for healing on the Sabbath and for claiming to be God's Son.

(2) **Read what Jesus said to these leaders in the following passage. Underline what they failed to do to experience life.**

"You pore over [diligently study (NIV)] the Scriptures because you think you have eternal life in them, yet they testify about Me. And you are not willing to come to Me that you may have life" (John 5:39-40).

These leaders were Scripture-centered. They diligently studied the Scriptures. That sounds commendable, doesn't it? But diligent Bible study was not enough. They needed a relationship with Jesus, and they refused to seek real life from Him. Being Scripture-centered can be one step shy of God's best. God's Word without a relationship with God can lead to a prideful and judgmental attitude, as these leaders had. They understood the letter of God's Word, but they didn't understand His Spirit. They needed a relationship with Jesus to experience the life God intended for them.

THE CHRIST-CENTERED APPROACH: THE WAY FOR US

What these leaders were missing is what we need. We *do* need to study the Scriptures diligently. Without them we will not know and correctly understand God's will and His ways. But we must not stop there. We need to move one more step into a relationship with Jesus Christ. The Holy Spirit takes God's Word and guides us to understand it correctly and apply it faithfully. Living for Christ and following Him are not just a set of rules and regulations to follow. He is a person. We follow Him. We live for Him, and He lives in us.

③ Match the description below with the correct approach to following Christ on the right in the margin. Write a letter beside each number.
___ 1. The way of the Pharisees
___ 2. The way of the Sadducees
___ 3. The way for us to follow
___ 4. Diligently studies Scriptures and comes to the Holy Spirit to understand and apply them in following Christ
___ 5. Diligently studies Scriptures, thinking they are the source of life rather than seeking a relationship with Jesus Christ
___ 6. Uses human reasoning and personal experience to decide what is right and wrong

④ If you had to identify the approach you have primarily used in following Christ up to this point, which one would it be—*a, b,* or *c?* Briefly explain your answer in the margin.

Now talk to Jesus. Describe the kind of relationship you want to have with Him. Pledge to study the Scriptures diligently and come to Him for life.

The Holy Spirit takes God's Word and guides us to understand it correctly and apply it faithfully.

a. Human-centered
b. Scripture-centered
c. Christ-centered

Answers: 1-b; 2-a; 3-c; 4-c; 5-b; 6-a

④ **Why?**

Day 5 • Introducing Six Disciplines

. . . .

↕ **Read and briefly meditate on "God's Word for Today" in the margin and respond to the Lord in prayer. Use the written prayer or pray your own.**

God's Word for Today

"Not that I have already reached the goal or am already fully mature, but I make every effort to take hold of it because I also have been taken hold of by Christ Jesus. Brothers, I do not consider myself to have taken hold of it. But one thing I do: forgetting what is behind and reaching forward to what is ahead, I pursue as my goal the prize promised by God's heavenly call in Christ Jesus."
Philippians 3:12-14

Today I want to introduce you to the six disciplines we will be studying and practicing during the coming weeks. Before I do that, let's talk about the word *disciplines*. That may be a word that makes you feel uncomfortable. It may stir up thoughts of painful and tiring work. For some people it may rouse feelings of a harsh, dry, lifeless legalism or a mindless routine. Let me put you at ease. That is not where we are heading.

Our primary focus is not on religious activity but a relationship with Jesus Christ—a love relationship that is real, joyful, meaningful, and fruitful. The six disciplines are activities and actions you can take to cultivate and strengthen your relationship with Christ. They will provide guidance for loving obedience to the will of Christ and meaning for your life that will result in joy and fruitfulness for the kingdom of Christ.

① **Based on the above descriptions, which of the following words describe what you should think about the disciplines? Check all that apply.**

○ harsh   ○ joyful   ○ loving obedience
○ love relationship   ○ legalistic   ○ fruitful
○ painful   ○ meaningful   ○ purposeful
○ tiring   ○ mindless routine   ○ uncomfortable
○ maturity   ○ strengthened   ○ a prize

Responding to the Lord

Lord, that describes me. I haven't yet reached the goal of full maturity in Christ, but I want to move in that direction. Help me forget my past failures and cleanse me of the sins of my past. Lord, clearly reveal to me the proper goal for my relationship with You and give me a passion to pursue that goal for Christ's sake. Amen.

If you checked *harsh, painful, tiring, legalistic, mindless routine,* or *uncomfortable,* you may want to go back and start today's lesson again. Those words should not be associated with these disciplines. Here's a brief introduction to the six disciplines we will study over the coming six weeks.

ABIDE IN CHRIST

To abide in Christ is central to all of the disciplines. Jesus invites you to a love relationship with Himself. He wants you to know, understand, and live according to His commands so that you can experience the best life God has to offer you. His Word and prayer are the tools through which we speak to Him and He speaks to us. By abiding in Christ, you receive all the life and vitality you need to be filled with joy and fruitfulness.

Optional Reading

Philippians 3

LIVE IN THE WORD

God has revealed Himself, His purposes, and His ways in the Bible. He has given guidelines for an abundant and meaningful life. Jesus set an example for us by knowing Scripture and applying it in His daily living. You will learn to read, study, memorize, and meditate on God's Word in order to know Him and understand His commands, His purposes, and His ways. Then you can live your life in a way that pleases Him and is abundantly full for you.

PRAY IN FAITH

Prayer is not just a religious activity; it describes a relationship with a person. Prayer is your intimate communion with God. In prayer you experience a loving relationship, you receive God's counsel and directions, you respond in praise and worship, you receive cleansing through confession, and you work together with God through petition for yourself and intercession for others.

FELLOWSHIP WITH BELIEVERS

When Jesus saved you, He placed you in the body of Christ with other believers. In relationships with other believers, you receive help to be all God wants you to be; and you are used by God to meet the needs of the rest of the body. Together we grow strong in our faith, and we accomplish the kingdom work of Christ in the world for which He died.

WITNESS TO THE WORLD

Jesus came with an assignment to seek and to save those who are lost. He went to the cross to reconcile a lost world to God the Father. He has given to us the ministry and message of reconciliation so that others may experience a saving relationship with God. We have both the privilege and responsibility to witness about Christ to a lost and dying world around us.

MINISTER TO OTHERS

Jesus modeled a life of service for His disciples and for us. He did not come to be served but to serve others. His call for us is to a life of service to those who are needy, both in the body of Christ and in the world that has yet to believe. When we love and serve others who are needy, we show our love for Christ Himself; and God uses that service to build up the body of Christ.

② Draw a star beside the discipline you most look forward to developing further. Circle the one for which you feel the most inadequate.

Ask Christ to enliven your walk with Him through these six disciplines.

Six Disciplines for New and Growing Believers
1. Abide in Christ
2. Live in the Word
3. Pray in Faith
4. Fellowship with Believers
5. Witness to the World
6. Minister to Others

Listen once again to Dámaris as she sings "The Call" (track 1) on the message-music CD.

Week 2 · **Abide in Christ**

"I am the vine, ye are the branches: He that abideth in me, and I in him, the same bringeth forth much fruit: for without me ye can do nothing" (John 15:5, KJV).

Abide in Christ

Live in a love relationship with Christ in which He fills you with His life and produces spiritual fruit through you for the Father's glory.

Abiding in Christ is central to all of the disciplines. Jesus invites you to a love relationship with Himself. He wants you to know, understand, and live according to His commands so that you can experience the best life God has to offer you. His Word and prayer are the tools through which we speak to Him and He speaks to us. By abiding in Christ, you receive all the life and vitality you need to be filled with joy and fruitfulness.

OVERVIEW OF WEEK 2
Day 1: Abiding in the Vine
Day 2: Experiencing Oneness with Christ
Day 3: Spending Time with the Master
Day 4: Bearing Spiritual Fruit
Day 5: Obeying Christ's Commands

VERSE TO MEMORIZE
"I am the vine, ye are the branches: He that abideth in me, and I in him, the same bringeth forth much fruit: for without me ye can do nothing" (John 15:5, KJV).

MESSAGE-MUSIC CD
"Moments with the Master" (track 2)

DISCIPLESHIP HELPS FOR WEEK 2
"The Disciple's Cross" (p. 93)

WHY THIS WEEK WILL BE MEANINGFUL TO YOU
You will understand how to abide in Christ and show your love for Christ by doing such things as …
- spending time with Christ in prayer;
- reading and obeying God's Word;
- accepting God's pruning and cleansing work;
- allowing Christ to work through you to produce spiritual fruit;
- choosing to become like Christ in your actions, attitudes, and thinking;
- submitting your will to His will and choosing to obey Him;
- loving others as Christ has loved you.

God's Word for Today

"I am the vine, you are the branches. He who abides in Me, and I in him, bears much fruit; for without Me you can do nothing."
John 15:5, NKJV

Responding in Prayer

Nothing? Lord, my pride wants to make a contribution, but I choose to agree with You. Apart from You I can do nothing of kingdom value. But I can be very fruitful in an abiding relationship with You. Show me how to have that kind of relationship with You and then enable me to live up to Your requirements. I'm a branch; You are the Vine. Be to me all I need. Amen.

Optional Reading

John 15

✳ *Abide:* continue in, dwell, remain, stand

Answers: 1-c; 2-c; 3-d; 4-b; 5-a; 6-a

Day 1 • Abiding in the Vine

Read "God's Word for Today" in the margin and respond to the Lord in prayer. Use the written prayer or pray your own. This week as your time permits, also consider the "Optional Readings." Today's reading includes Jesus' parable about the Vine. I'll guide you to read it below.

1. John 15:5 is your Scripture-memory verse for this week. Use the memory card for John 15:5 and the tips on page 92 to begin memorizing it.

The word *abide* is not used very much these days. *To abide** means *to continue in, to dwell, to remain, or to stand.* But even those words seem inadequate to describe what Jesus means by abiding in Him. Jesus told the parable of the Vine to make His meaning more clear. Just as a branch is connected to a grapevine, He wants us to be solidly connected to Him. The illustration of a vine and its branches reveals these truths and more:
• The vine and the branch are of the same substance, the same wood.
• A branch that is grafted into the vine sends fibers down into the vine. The vine sends fibers into the branch until they become one.
• The branch needs the vine in order to live. It cannot survive without the sap from the vine.
• The vine needs the branch in order to bear fruit. Without the branch the vine cannot produce fruit by itself.

2. Turn in your Bible to John 15:1-17. Read the parable and underline verses that are particularly meaningful or that you would like to memorize. Then match the truth on the left with the correct person on the right. Write a letter beside each number.

___ 1. Bears fruit, more fruit, much fruit   a. Jesus
___ 2. Can do nothing by himself   b. God the Father
___ 3. Gets cut off and thrown into the fire   c. Disciples/followers
___ 4. The Vine Keeper who prunes the branches   d. Branch with no fruit
___ 5. The Vine that produces fruit through the branches
___ 6. One who chose and appointed the branches to bear fruit

We will learn more from this parable this week. "Abide in Christ" describes a love relationship you develop with your Savior. The depth and strength and joy of that relationship grow as you spend time with Christ learning from Him, becoming like Him, receiving from Him, and obeying Him.

🎧 As you read the words below, listen to Dámaris sing "Moments with the Master" (track 2) on the message-music CD. Underline reasons you would want to spend time with Jesus, your Master. I've underlined one.

In my moments with the Master / Sitting at His feet
The blessings are abundant / The fellowship is sweet
<u>I find the strength and wisdom</u> / Everything I need
In the presence of my Lord

In my moments with the Master / He takes on my concerns
With tender reassurance / And the comfort of His Word
His mercy leaves me breathless / Longing to return
To the presence of my Lord

Chorus
He feeds my spirit / Guides my way / Shepherds me to the pasture
I look forward every day / To my moments with the Master

In my moments with the Master / My heart bowed in prayer
His truth, a holy treasure / He offers to me there
It's like the peace of heaven / The solitude we share
I could never ask for more
   Repeat chorus
In my moments with the Master / Sitting at His feet
The blessings are abundant / The fellowship is sweet
I find the strength and wisdom / Everything I need
In the presence of my Lord / As He leads me to the pasture
In my moments with the Master

③ What is your attitude toward spending time with your Master in prayer and reading His Word? Check one.
   ○ a. I enjoy time with Christ and look forward to it daily.
   ○ b. I dread taking time to pray and read God's Word.
         I find it very difficult to do.
   ○ c. Based on past experience, I've not been very interested
         in time with my Master.
   ○ d. I want Christ to increase my desire for time with Him
         so that the words of this song will be true for me.

Spend time with your Master in prayer. Ask Him to teach you to abide.

Day 2 • Experiencing Oneness with Christ

God's Word for Today

"If anyone loves Me, he will keep My word; and My Father will love him, and We will come to him and make Our home with him."
John 14:23, NKJV

Read and briefly meditate on "God's Word for Today" in the margin and respond to the Lord in prayer. Use the written prayer or pray your own.

Can you believe that Jesus and the Heavenly Father want to come and make their home with you? They do! To abide in Christ, you love and obey Him, and He takes up residence in your life.

Jesus set an example for us to follow in abiding. He had a oneness with His Father. This oneness was so intimate that to know one was to know both. Jesus said to His disciples, "If you know Me, you will also know My Father" (John 14:7). But when Philip asked Jesus to show them the Father, Jesus said that He had already shown them the Father through His words and works:

Responding in Prayer

Lord, I love You. And this is a promise I would love to experience fully: You and the Father coming to live with me. But I see the condition: I need to keep Your word. Lord, I want to do just that. I need Your help. Father, I ask You in Jesus' name to draw me into this love relationship for Your glory. Amen.

> Jesus said to him, "Have I been among you all this time without your knowing Me, Philip? The one who has seen Me has seen the Father. How can you say, 'Show us the Father'? Don't you believe that I am in the Father and the Father is in Me? The words I speak to you I do not speak on My own. The Father who lives in Me does His works. Believe Me that I am in the Father and the Father is in Me" (John 14:9-11).

1. **Answer the following questions based on Jesus' words above.**
   Where was the Father in relationship to Jesus and Jesus to the Father?

   _____

   Where did Jesus' words and works come from? _____

Optional Reading

John 14

Jesus was in the Father, and the Father was in Jesus. That's a mystery, isn't it? Jesus didn't speak on His own initiative; He spoke the words the Father gave Him. He didn't work on His own; the Father worked through Him. Jesus said similar things on several occasions making clear that His works and words came from the Father. (Read the Scriptures under "Jesus' Words and Work" in the right-page margin.)

John 15:4
"Remain in Me, and I in you."

John 15:7
"If you remain in Me and My words remain in you, ask whatever you want and it will be done for you."

Just as Jesus had a oneness with the Father, He wants us to experience that same oneness with Him. He wants to be in us, and He wants us to live in Him (John 15:4). He wants His words to abide in us (John 15:7), and He explained that we cannot do anything apart from Him (John 15:4-5). Any fruit we bear comes because of His working in us and through us. This doesn't mean we are passive and uninvolved. It means that we allow God to set the agenda and give the assignment. Then we depend on His Holy Spirit to empower and enable us to do what He desires.

This intimate love relationship and oneness with Jesus Christ are the basis for abiding in Christ. This discipline is not just a set of religious activities you *do*. It describes a *relationship* you have with a person—Jesus Christ.

(2) **Mark the following statements T for true or F for false.**
_____ 1. Jesus desires a relationship with me in which He lives in me and works through me to produce spiritual fruit.
_____ 2. The better I abide in Christ, the more people will see Jesus in me.
_____ 3. He didn't really mean I can do nothing of kingdom value without Him. By hard work and much effort I can produce fruit for Him.
_____ 4. If I love Jesus, I will choose to obey Him.

(Answers: T-1,2,4; F-3)

"Abide in Christ" is the central discipline and has a connection to all of the other disciplines we will study in this course. And the other disciplines help to strengthen your abiding in Christ. Without this relationship with Christ, however, the other disciplines are meaningless. Together they help you grow toward spiritual maturity and a balanced life of discipleship.

(3) **Turn to page 93 and study the Disciple's Cross diagram from** *MasterLife*. **As you learned last week, the call to discipleship is a call to deny self, take up your cross, and follow Him. Notice that Abiding in Christ is at the center of a disciple's life. Jesus must be Lord. Live in the Word and Pray in Faith help you develop your vertical relationship with God. Fellowship with Believers and Witness to the World help you develop your horizontal relationships with others. And the variety of ministries are ways you show the love of Christ as you Minister to Others.**

(4) **What is the central and most important discipline in a disciple's life?**

_____

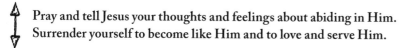

Pray and tell Jesus your thoughts and feelings about abiding in Him. Surrender yourself to become like Him and to love and serve Him.

John 15:4-5
"Just as a branch is unable to produce fruit by itself unless it remains on the vine, so neither can you unless you remain in Me. … The one who remains in Me and I in him produces much fruit, because you can do nothing without Me."

Jesus' Words and Work
"The Son is not able to do anything on His own, but only what He sees the Father doing" (John 5:19).

"I can do nothing on My own. … I do not seek My own will, but the will of Him who sent Me" (John 5:30).

"My teaching isn't Mine but is from the One who sent Me" (John 7:16).

"I do nothing on My own. But just as the Father taught Me, I say these things" (John 8:28).

"I have not spoken on My own, but the Father Himself who sent Me has given Me a command as to what I should say and what I should speak. … So the things that I speak, I speak just as the Father has told Me" (John 12:49-50).

God's Word for Today

"If you abide in Me, and My words abide in you, you will ask what you desire, and it shall be done for you."
John 15:7, NKJV

Responding in Prayer

Now that's a promise! Help me abide in You in such a way that I know You and Your desires. Cause Your words to live in me. Teach me how to have this kind of relationship with You so that I can have power with You in prayer—power that brings You credit and glory, not me. Amen.

Optional Reading

John 16

Listen once again to Dámaris as she sings "Moments with the Master" (track 2) on the message-music CD.

Day 3 • Spending Time with the Master

Read and briefly meditate on "God's Word for Today" in the margin and respond to the Lord in prayer. Use the written prayer or pray your own.

If we are to abide in Christ, we must take time to be with Him. We need to listen to Him speak through His Word and prayer. We need to surrender our lives to God's work of molding and shaping us into the image of His Son.

JESUS SPENT TIME WITH HIS FATHER

We want to follow the example of Christ. Prayer is not just a religious activity you complete and check off your to-do list. Prayer is a relationship with God. Jesus taught His disciples to pray, but the teaching began as they watched Him devote Himself to prayer. They observed as Jesus spent time with His Father in prayer, and then they saw the fruit of the prayers in what Jesus said and did.

1. **Read the Scriptures below and underline some of the places Jesus prayed.**

"He [Jesus] often withdrew to deserted places and prayed" (Luke 5:16).

"During those days He went out to the mountain to pray and spent all night in prayer to God" (Luke 6:12).

"Very early in the morning, while it was still dark, He got up, went out, and made His way to a deserted place. And He was praying there" (Mark 1:35).

"After He said good-bye to them, He went away to the mountain to pray. When evening came … He was alone on the land" (Mark 6:46-47).

2. **What time of day did Jesus pray? Check all that apply.**
   ○ a. early morning   ○ b. late night   ○ c. other times during the day

Jesus met His Father in the early morning for prayer. At other times He prayed during the day or at night—sometimes all night. Jesus frequently chose places (whether mountain or desert) where He could be alone with His Father when He prayed. But at other times He prayed with people around Him. He was praying during His baptism when the Holy Spirit descended on Him like a dove (Luke 3:21-22). He prayed in private with His disciples and then revealed to them for the first time that He would suffer and be killed by religious leaders (Luke 9:18-22). Later He took Peter, James, and John onto a mountain to pray; and these three witnessed the transfiguration (Luke 9:28-36).

Jesus prayed to understand His Father's will about where He preached and ministered (Mark 1:35-39). He spent all night praying before He chose the twelve disciples whom He named apostles (Luke 6:12-16). Critical decisions like these required much prayer. Jesus said, "I have not spoken on My own, but the Father Himself who sent Me has given Me a command as to what I should say and what I should speak" (John 12:49). Jesus received the words He spoke and taught while in prayer with His Father.

③ If Jesus, the Son of God, needed to spend time with His Father in order know and do His will, do you think you need to spend time with your Heavenly Father and Master to know and do His will? Check one.
○ a. No, I've got my act together, and I can manage life by myself.
○ b. Yes indeed. If the Master of the universe is willing to personally guide my life, I know I need Him. I'd love to spend time with Him.

CULTIVATING A LOVE RELATIONSHIP WITH GOD

When I was in the eighth grade, my science teacher took me arrowhead hunting. We gathered enough Native American artifacts to fill a sack—and I was hooked! I found some sites near my home, and I spent hours walking the plowed fields looking for artifacts. My mind wasn't too busy during those hours, so I often found myself talking to God about everything going on in my life. I would talk to Him about problems I was facing, decisions I needed to make, and relationships that needed help. I asked Him to reveal His will or give directions so that I could follow Him. Sometimes I reviewed all of His blessings to me and gave thanks. I praised Him for the beauty of His creation and expressed my love for Him. As I spent time with my Heavenly Father, He cultivated a deep and abiding love relationship with me. That kind of relationship comes only with time. It can't develop with only brief moments.

 Get alone with your Heavenly Father sometime this week. Choose a quiet place where you are not likely to be interrupted. If weather and your health permit, go to a favorite place outside. Spend at least half an hour (more if you can). Take time to talk to Him about all of the things going on in your life. Worship, praise, and thank Him. Take time to enjoy His presence. Be still and know that He is your God. After your moments with the Father, write a few words in the margin describing what you felt and thought. Did you sense that He spoke to you? If so, write that down, too.

Prayer is not just a religious activity you complete and check off your to-do list. Prayer is a relationship with God.

My Time with My Heavenly Father

God's Word for Today

"By this My Father is glorified, that you bear much fruit; so you will be My disciples."
John 15:8, NKJV

Responding in Prayer

Father, I want my life to bring you glory. I want to bear much fruit. Jesus, show me how to follow You and receive from You (my Vine) all I need to be fruitful for the Father's glory. Amen.

Optional Reading

Galatians 5:16-26

Romans 8:28-29, NIV
"In all things God works for the good of those who love him, who have been called according to his purpose. For those God foreknew he also predestined to be conformed to the likeness of his Son, that he might be the firstborn among many brothers."

Day 4 • Bearing Spiritual Fruit

Read and briefly meditate on "God's Word for Today" in the margin and respond to the Lord in prayer. Use the written prayer or pray your own.

Jesus wants you to bear much fruit that will bring glory to the Father. Glory is the evidence that God has accomplished a significant work in you. One way God works in you to produce fruit is molding and shaping you to be like Christ. "We all, with unveiled faces, are reflecting the glory of the Lord and are being transformed into the same image from glory to glory; this is from the Lord who is the Spirit" (2 Corinthians 3:18). God wants you to be like Jesus. The branch and the Vine become one—the Vine in the branch and the branch in the Vine. In Galatians Paul described spiritual fruit that the Holy Spirit produces in the life of a person who is surrendered to the Spirit's control.

(1) **If you haven't read today's "Optional Reading," turn to the passage in your Bible and read it now. Underline the fruit of the Spirit. Then rate yourself on the extent to which your life reflects each fruit. Use the following scale and write a number from 0 to 10 beside each part of the Spirit's fruit.**

0 = This is not present in my life.
3 = Budding fruit—I see it coming!
5 = Fruit is present but needs to mature.
7 = The fruit is looking good (thank God), but occasionally I fail.
10 = Isn't God amazing? Look what He has done.

____ love	____ patience	____ faith
____ joy	____ kindness	____ gentleness
____ peace	____ goodness	____ self-control

PRUNING REQUIRED

Jesus is in heaven now, but our world still needs to know Him. We have His teachings in Scripture, but God also intends to reveal Christ to a watching world through the body of Christ—the church—and the members of that body. So God is working to make you look, think, and act like Jesus. In our parable of the Vine, God is the Vine Keeper or Husbandman who prunes the branch so that it will be more fruitful. Though pruning may be painful in the short term, the good and loving goal of the Father is to make you very fruitful for His glory.

(2) **Read Romans 8:28-29 in the margin and underline what God uses for your good to shape you into the image of His Son.**

God uses "all things" to work for your good. He uses the Scriptures to reveal what Jesus is like so that you can make adjustments by choice. He can use good things to encourage and strengthen you. But He also uses the difficult, bad, and even evil things that may happen to you to accomplish good in your life. Like a sculptor removing pieces of marble to reveal the angel he's carving, God chips away everything in your life, mind, and behavior that doesn't look like Jesus. Knowing that in the end you can be more like Jesus will help you endure the times of trial that may come.

Sometimes I have had more things to do than I could manage. Even too many good things can overwhelm me at times. I've learned in times like that to pray and ask my heavenly Vine Keeper to prune my life. I ask Him to reveal to me the things that need to go, the things I need to quit or give up. He wants me to be more fruitful, so I trust Him to remove what is not best. You may want to keep that in mind for a time when you have more than you can handle.

GOSPEL FRUIT

The ultimate fruit God is looking for from the branches are the souls of men and women who come to Christ in a spiritual harvest. Jesus, the true Vine, said of Himself, "The Son of Man has come to seek and to save the lost" (Luke 19:10). Then He gave the same assignment to His disciples: "As the Father has sent Me, I also send you" (John 20:21). Paul wrote to the church at Colosse to commend them for their fruit: "All over the world this gospel is bearing fruit and growing, just as it has been doing among you since the day you heard it and understood God's grace in all its truth" (Colossians 1:6, NIV).

③ Read "One Object of the Branch" by Andrew Murray in the right margin. Then finish the following statement: "The heavenly Vine and the branch, have equally their place in the world exclusively for one purpose, to …

_____ ."

Abiding in Christ is not just for the benefit of the branch. Yes, the branch receives sap from the Vine to grow strong. But this is for one purpose: to bear fruit by bringing men and women to the Savior. We will work on this further in week 6 as we focus on your "witness to the world."

Thank God for the person who helped you come to know Jesus as your Savior. Ask the Lord to use you to bear fruit by bringing others to Him. Ask God to continually change you to be more and more like Jesus.

One Object of the Branch

"It is because Christians do not understand or accept this truth, that they so fail in their efforts and prayers to live the branch life. They often desire it very earnestly; they read and meditate and pray, and yet they fail, they wonder why? The reason is very simple: they do not know that fruit-bearing is the one thing they have been saved for. Just as entirely as Christ became the true Vine with the one object, you have been made a branch too, with the one object of bearing fruit for the salvation of men. The Vine and the branch are equally under the unchangeable law of fruit-bearing as the one reason of their being. Christ and the believer, the heavenly Vine and the branch, have equally their place in the world exclusively for one purpose, to carry God's saving love to men."

Andrew Murray, *The True Vine* (Chicago: Moody Press, n.d.), 21.

Day 5 • Obeying Christ's Commands

God's Word for Today

"If you keep My commandments, you will abide in My love, just as I have kept My Father's commandments and abide in His love."
John 15:10, NKJV

Responding in Prayer

Lord Jesus, You've given me a perfect example of obedience. You have kept the Father's commands. Since You command that of me, I trust that You can enable me to do it. I want to obey You. I want to please You. I want to abide in Your perfect and fully satisfying love. Make Your commandments clear to me, and I will obey. Amen.

Optional Reading

Matthew 7

↕ **Read and briefly meditate on "God's Word for Today" in the margin and respond to the Lord in prayer. Use the written prayer or pray your own.**

When God first placed Adam and Eve in the garden, He gave them only one command. He wanted obedience from His creation. Yet they rebelled against God's command, and sin entered the world. That broken relationship separated humans from their Creator. Jesus restored our opportunity to have a right relationship with God through His obedience on the cross. Paul tells us, "Just as through one man's disobedience the many were made sinners, so also through the one man's obedience the many will be made righteous" (Romans 5:19). Christ's obedience opened the way. In "God's Word for Today" Jesus explained that obedience and love go together.

1 **Read John 15:10 again ("God's Word for Today"). What must you do to live in Christ's love?**

_____

God created you and has called you to a love relationship with Himself. You show your love for Him by your obedience to His commands. Jesus modeled that loving obedience in His own life with the Father by keeping the Father's commandments (John 15:10). When we obey, we receive the reward of abiding in the Savior's love.

2 **Read the following Scriptures and answer the question that follows.**

"If you love Me, you will keep My commandments" (John 14:15).

"The one who has My commands and keeps them is the one who loves Me. And the one who loves Me will be loved by My Father. I also will love him and will reveal Myself to him. If anyone loves Me, he will keep My word. My Father will love him, and We will come to him and make Our home with him. The one who doesn't love Me will not keep My words" (John 14:21,23-24).

3 **Who is the one who loves Jesus Christ? Check one.**
○ a. The one who obeys Christ's commands
○ b. The one who does not obey Christ's commands

You show your love for Christ through obedience. Lack of obedience is an indication that you don't love Him as you should. Though your obedience may fall short of perfect, God looks at your heart. In those matters where you clearly know His will, do you choose to obey Him?

(4) **How would you evaluate your love for Christ? Check a response or write your own.**
   ○ a. I deeply love my Savior, and I choose to obey Him.
   ○ b. I say I love Him with my lips, but my obedience says I don't love Him.
   ○ c. I need to grow in both my obedience and my love.
   ○ d. Other: _____

Sometimes obedience to Christ will be costly. As your love for Christ grows, the capacity for sacrificial obedience will also grow. Through His obedience Jesus set an example for us to follow. He loved the Father enough to go to the cross in obedience (see Philippians 2:8 in the margin).

LOVING ONE ANOTHER
God has given many commands throughout Scripture. Once, when He was asked what the greatest command was, Jesus summed up all the commands by saying we should love God and love our neighbor (see Matthew 22:37-40). In the parable of the Vine Jesus gave one special command: "This is My command: love one another as I have loved you. No one has greater love than this, that someone would lay down his life for his friends" (John 15:12-13). Jesus went on the next day to lay down His life for His friends, demonstrating His love. Earlier in the evening Jesus spoke about loving one another when He said, "By this all people will know that you are My disciples, if you have love for one another" (John 13:35).

In the weeks to come, I want to help you obey these commands. You will learn to love others by praying for them. As you fellowship with believers and witness to the world, you will learn to show God's love by meeting needs. In a variety of ministries you will demonstrate love to those inside and outside the fellowship of believers. Abiding in Christ will strengthen you for this kind of love. Do you see how these disciplines work together?

Talk to the Lord about your love and obedience. Give Him permission to prune you to make you more fruitful. Ask Him to increase your capacity to love others in the way He loved. As time permits, spend some moments with your Master and enjoy His sweet fellowship!

Philippians 2:8
"He humbled Himself
   by becoming obedient
to the point of death—
   even to death on a cross."

Matthew 22:37-40
"'Love the Lord your God
with all your heart, with
all your soul, and with
all your mind.' This is the
greatest and most important
commandment. The second
is like it: 'Love your neighbor
as yourself.' All the Law
and the Prophets depend on
these two commandments."

Listen once again to Dámaris as she sings "Moments with the Master" (track 2) on the message-music CD.

Week 3 · **Live in the Word**

"Be doers of the word and not hearers only, deceiving yourselves" (James 1:22).

Live in the Word

Read, study, memorize, and meditate on God's Word to know Him and understand His commands, His purposes, and His ways. Then you can live your life in a way that pleases God and is abundantly full for you.

God has revealed Himself, His purposes, and His ways in the Bible. He has given guidelines for an abundant and meaningful life. Jesus set an example for us by knowing Scripture and applying it in His daily living.

OVERVIEW OF WEEK 3
Day 1: Treasuring God's Word
Day 2: Reading God's Word
Day 3: Memorizing God's Word
Day 4: Studying God's Word
Day 5: Doing God's Word

VERSE TO MEMORIZE
"Be doers of the word and not hearers only, deceiving yourselves" (James 1:22).

MESSAGE-MUSIC CD
"Live in Your Word" (track 3)

DISCIPLESHIP HELPS FOR WEEK 3
"Bible Study Tools" (pp. 94-95)

WHY THIS WEEK WILL BE MEANINGFUL TO YOU
You will understand how to read and study God's Word to know God's will and His ways. Then you will show your love for Him and His Word by doing such things as …
   • memorizing and meditating on meaningful verses of Scripture;
   • reading and studying God's Word on a regular basis;
   • taking specific steps of obedience to God's will as revealed in His Word;
   • adjusting your behavior and your character to reflect God's character
     and His ways as He has revealed them in Scripture.

Day 1 • Treasuring God's Word

 Read and briefly meditate on "God's Word for Today" in the margin and respond to the Lord in prayer. As your time permits each day this week, read the Scripture for "Optional Reading" listed in the margin. This week's "Optional Reading" comes from Psalm 119. This chapter has much to say about the value of God's Word. As you read it in your Bible, mark verses that are particularly meaningful or that you would like to memorize. As you read, you may want to pause and talk to God about what you are reading. Cultivate your relationship with Him as you listen to Him speak through His Word.

Responding in Prayer
Holy Father, I live in a world that is filled with impurities at every turn. Keeping my way pure in such a world seems almost impossible to me. But I know Jesus was able to live a pure life. Since He lives in me, I'm trusting Him to guide me by His Spirit and according to Your Word to help me live my life in a way that pleases You. I need Your help, and I ask for it in Jesus' name. Amen.

The Bible is a treasure book that is your authoritative source for faith and a trustworthy guide for godly living. God has revealed Himself, His purposes, and His ways in the Bible. He has given guidelines for an abundant and meaningful life.

 Read the following Scripture and underline the words or phrases that describe the value of God's words. I've underlined one for you.

Optional Reading
Psalm 119:1-32

Psalm 19:7-11
"The instruction of the LORD is perfect, reviving the soul;
the testimony of the LORD is trustworthy, making the
    inexperienced wise.
The precepts of the LORD are right, <u>making the heart glad</u>;
the commandment of the LORD is radiant, making the eyes light up.
The fear of the LORD is pure, enduring forever;
the ordinances of the LORD are reliable and altogether righteous.
They are more desirable than gold—than an abundance of pure gold;
and sweeter than honey—than honey dripping from the comb.
In addition, Your servant is warned by them;
there is great reward in keeping them."

God's words are trustworthy, perfect, right, radiant, pure, enduring, reliable,
righteous, desirable, and sweeter than honey! They can revive you, make you
wise and glad, and enlighten you. They can warn you for your own protection.
When you obey them, "there is great reward." So this week I want to help you
live *in* God's Word AND live *by* God's Word.

God's words are trustworthy, perfect, right, radiant, pure, enduring, reliable, righteous, desirable, and sweeter than honey!

🎧 As you read the words to "Live in Your Word" below, listen to Dámaris sing it on track 3 of the message-music CD.

Chaos ahead, choices to make / It's silence I need
Seeking to know Your heart and Your mind / Where You want to lead
Father, I thirst for Your wisdom / Make me at home in Your truth
I want to …

Chorus
Live in Your Word / Abiding in faith / I want to walk in Your steps
To trust and obey / A light upon the narrow path / A lamp unto my feet
I want to live in Your Word / 'Til Your Word is living in me.

I need Your Word buried like seeds / Deep in my soul
Chapter and verse, nourishing me / A harvest will grow
Oh, Father. You feed every hunger / I know where my strength is found
So I will …
   Repeat chorus
You spoke and the universe came to be
You speak and my life has endless possibilities / So I will …
   Repeat chorus

② Reflect on the following values and benefits of God's Word mentioned in the song. Check two or three benefits that are the most meaningful to you or most needed by you today.

○ a. to know His heart and mind   ○ e. to light the narrow path
○ b. to know where He wants to lead   ○ f. to be a lamp to my feet
○ c. to have His wisdom   ○ g. to nourish me
○ d. to know the truth   ○ h. to produce a spiritual harvest

God's Word is intended to point you to Him for a relationship with the Author. His Holy Spirit can help you apply His Word so that you can gain all the benefits God has in store for you. Reading and studying God's Word need to include prayer as well. The knowledge of God's Word and the relationship to Him in prayer go together. So …

 Talk to the Lord. Ask Him to give you the desire to know and do all He reveals to you in Scripture. Ask Him to help you live in His Word in such a way that His Word will live in you.

Live in Your Word

God's Word is intended to point you to Him for a relationship with the Author.

Day 2 • Reading God's Word

God's Word for Today

"All Scripture is inspired by God and is profitable for teaching, for rebuking, for correcting, for training in righteousness, so that the man of God may be complete, equipped for every good work."
2 Timothy 3:16–17

Responding in Prayer

Lord, I want to be mature, complete, and equipped by You for good works. Thank You for giving me Your Word. Cause me to treasure it. I pray that You will teach me through the Scriptures. Rebuke and correct me when necessary and train me to live in a right way—one that pleases You and is absolutely best for me. Amen.

Optional Reading

Psalm 119:33–64

The Bible is filled with knowledge and wisdom straight from our Creator.

Psalm 119:105
"Your word is a lamp
    for my feet
and a light on my path."

 Read and briefly meditate on "God's Word for Today" in the margin and respond to the Lord in prayer. Use the written prayer or pray your own.

The summer before I entered high school, I attended a Christian conference with my family. My teacher for the week, Dan Griffin, challenged me to begin reading my Bible every day. He described the value of knowing what God had to say to me to guide my life according to His plans and ways. I decided to do it! I went to the bookstore and bought a new Bible, and I began a journey in God's Word that would deeply shape my life.

Throughout my high-school years, I read at least a chapter a day. I loved the Lord, and I wanted to know how to live my life in a way that would please Him. Once I knew what God wanted me to do and not do, those things became my desires. During those years I became a student of God's Word. At the same time, God drew me to Himself in prayer. I spent time talking to Him about everything in my life. Through that combination of reading God's Word and having a prayer relationship with the Author, God began shaping and guiding my life as a follower of Jesus Christ. His Word became a light to my path (see Psalm 119:105).

1. **Where are you in your relationship with God through the reading of His Word? Check a response or write your own.**
   ○ a. I am already regularly reading God's Word .
   ○ b. I am ready to start that wonderful journey of reading God's Word.
   ○ c. I'm weak in that desire. Lord, please help and encourage me.
   ○ d. Other:_____

The Bible is filled with knowledge and wisdom straight from our Creator. In the Bible you read about God and how He relates to people. You learn from the examples of others—both examples of things to avoid and models to follow. The Bible is God's guidebook for living life to the fullest measure—to experience the life for which God created you. But if that wealth of information never gets from the pages of your Bible into your mind, it is of no value to you.

As you seek to follow Christ, you learn about Him by reading the Bible. You read how He lived and the way He related to people so that you can follow His example. You read the words He preached and taught. And then you can read the words of His first followers as they gave instruction to others about how to follow Him. If you have not already done so, decide today to give priority to reading, studying, and applying God's Word to your life.

(2) **Suppose that your best friend asked you why he or she should read God's Word. In a sentence or two, write what you would say.**

_____

_____

When you read God's Word, watch for insights that should be of special interest to you. Mark your Bible so that you can review key thoughts. I have a key (or a code) in the front of the Bible I read from daily. As I find verses, words, phrases, or illustrations that are meaningful, I underline them and place a letter (or code) in the margin so that I can review those insights later.

For instance, I identify commands to obey and mark them with a _C_. Sins to avoid are marked with an _S_. You can mark prayers you can pray— praise, thanksgiving, petition, or intercession. Identify examples you can follow. Mark names of God or descriptions that teach you about who He is and what He does. Underline principles for living. Each time you open God's Word, you will mine gems and nuggets of truth that can guide your living.

(3) **Read the key to some of my codes in the margin. Circle a few of the letters or codes that you think might be meaningful to you. If you want to use such a system for your own Bible reading, make up your own codes. You might even make a bookmark as a quick reference for your codes.**

(4) **Turn in your Bible to Ephesians 1:3-12. Try out your codes by reading and marking some of these special truths in the margin of your Bible.**

(5) **Write below or in the margin one code and the truth you marked in Ephesians 1:3-12 that was particularly meaningful to you.**

_____

↕ Ephesians 1:3-12 can be the basis for a wonderful prayer time of thanksgiving for all of the things God has done for you. Close today's study with a time of prayer, thanking God for every spiritual blessing. Use your Bible as you pray.

Suggested Codes for Marking Your Bible

A	attribute of God
C	command to obey
CT	character trait to develop
E	example to follow
EA	example to avoid
F	faith to emulate
IP	intercessory prayer to pray for others
N	name of God
P1	praise to offer
P2	petition to ask
PC	promise to claim
PR	principle for living
S	sin to confess or avoid
T	thanksgiving to offer
TR	truth to confess
W	warning to heed

Day 3 • Memorizing God's Word

 Read and briefly meditate on "God's Word for Today" in the margin and respond to the Lord in prayer. Use the written prayer or pray your own.

Jesus set an example for us to follow with regard to God's Word. He knew His Father's will and often quoted Scripture. He quoted Scripture when Satan tempted Him. At other times He quoted Scripture in His teaching or to explain why He was taking a particular course of action. He not only knew the Scriptures, but He also lived His life by them.

① **Turn in your Bible to Matthew 4:1-11 and read about Satan's temptation of Jesus. Underline the Scriptures Jesus quoted as He resisted these temptations. And watch out—Satan also quoted Scripture.**

First Satan tempted Jesus in the area of His fleshly appetite, appealing to Jesus' hunger after His fast. Jesus responded by quoting Deuteronomy 8:3: "Man must not live on bread alone but on every word that comes from the mouth of God." Notice that feeding on God's Word can be more important than eating. Sometimes you may want to follow His example and fast (go without eating for a while) in order to devote time to prayer and reading God's Word.

In his second temptation of Jesus, Satan quoted Psalm 91:11-12. He was attempting to get Jesus to gain acceptance and recognition among the religious leaders at the temple through this spectacular demonstration. Knowing Scripture alone, however, is not always sufficient. Satan quoted the words correctly, but he appealed to the wrong motives. Jesus corrected him by quoting Deuteronomy 6:16: "Do not test the Lord your God." The more you know of God's Word and spend time with Him seeking to understand it, the more likely you will be able to apply it correctly. His Holy Spirit in you can help you know and do His will correctly.

② **What was one primary benefit Jesus had from knowing God's Word?**
 ○ a. He could show off His knowledge and impress people.
 ○ b. He could carry on a good argument on religious subjects.
 ○ c. He could resist temptation and avoid sin.

Many people diligently study the Bible for the knowledge they gain to impress people or win arguments. Knowing the truth is valuable, but these are not very good motives. Jesus' benefit in Matthew 4 was that He knew His Father's will and chose to resist temptation and not sin against His Father.

Satan's third temptation of Jesus was an appeal to get Him to try achieving redemption and His kingdom rule over the world without having to go to the cross. Essentially, Satan was saying, "There's an easier way." Again, Jesus resisted the temptation to sin by quoting Scripture. This time He quoted Deuteronomy 6:13. After that encounter the Devil gave up tempting Jesus for a while. Do you want to resist temptation and keep yourself from sin? Then spend time hiding God's Word in your mind and heart.

③ **Read again "God's Word for Today" (Psalm 119:11) in the margin on page 38. What is one good reason to memorize God's Word?**

_____

Knowing God's Word helps you know right from wrong according to God's standards, not man's. Knowing God's will and ways, you can choose what is right. Jesus applied His knowledge of Scripture in His ministry so that He would fulfill prophecies about Him. For instance, one day Jesus asked His disciples to fetch the colt of a donkey for Him to ride into Jerusalem. His disciples later realized, "This took place so that what was spoken through the prophet might be fulfilled" (Matthew 21:4).

④ **Read Matthew 21:5 in the margin and compare it to the quotation from the prophet Zechariah in Zechariah 9:9.**

Jesus lived His life in fulfillment of the Scriptures. Jesus also used Scripture to evaluate what was taking place in the temple courts. He condemned the religious leaders for their failure to be the people God intended. "He said to them, 'It is written, "My house will be called a house of prayer." But you are making it "a den of thieves!"'" (Matthew 21:13). He was quoting from Isaiah 56:7 and Jeremiah 7:11. Scripture is valuable for instruction and correction.

⑤ **Start memorizing James 1:22. Use your Scripture-memory card and the tips on page 92. Review John 15:5 from last week.**

✢ **Thank God for His Word that reveals His will and ways. Ask Him to guide you to learn His Word and apply it correctly so that you will not sin against Him and so that you will become a doer of the Word and not just a hearer.**

Deuteronomy 6:13, NIV
"Fear the LORD your God, serve him only."

Knowing God's Word helps you know right from wrong according to God's standards, not man's.

Matthew 21:5
"See, your King is coming
     to you,
gentle, and mounted
     on a donkey,
even on a colt, the foal
     of a beast of burden."

Zechariah 9:9
"See, your King is coming
     to you;
He is righteous and
     victorious,
humble and riding
     on a donkey,
on a colt, the foal of a donkey."

Day 4 • Studying God's Word

God's Word for Today

"Be diligent to present yourself approved to God, a worker who doesn't need to be ashamed, correctly teaching the word of truth."
2 Timothy 2:15

"Study to shew thyself approved unto God, a workman that needeth not to be ashamed, rightly dividing the word of truth."
2 Timothy 2:15, KJV

Responding in Prayer

Lord, I want to have Your approval. I don't want to be ashamed. I have so much to learn about Your "word of truth." Please help me know how to study Your Word diligently. Then encourage me to be diligent in my study. Amen.

Optional Reading

Psalm 119:105-144

"The best commentary on the Bible is the Bible."

Read and briefly meditate on "God's Word for Today" in the margin and respond to the Lord in prayer. Use the written prayer or pray your own.

Reading God's Word is a good starting point to know what God has said and what He has revealed about Himself. Meditating on His Word and committing it to memory take you deeper still. In "God's Word for Today," Paul encourages you to go another step deeper by diligently studying God's Word. Digging deeper into God's Word through Bible study brings greater understanding and may clarify the appropriate application of the truths you have read. Today I want to introduce you to several tools and approaches to Bible study.

1. Turn to page 94 and read about the types of Bible study tools that may help you in your study of Scripture. Then match the tool (left) with its description (right).

___ 1. translation   a. list of words with Bible references to their use

___ 2. concordance   b. maps and helps to study geography

___ 3. reference   c. defines Bible words, concepts, topics, people, history, and/or geography

___ 4. study Bible   d. book explaining the meaning of Bible texts

___ 5. dictionary   e. Bible text translated to make language clear

___ 6. commentary   f. Bible with many study tools included

___ 7. atlas   g. note listing another reference for a word or phrase

(Answers: 1-e; 2-a; 3-g; 4-f; 5-c; 6-d; 7-b)

STUDY THE BIBLE ITSELF

Someone has said, "The best commentary on the Bible is the Bible." You can read one passage from Paul and understand a truth from Scripture. But suppose you then read what Jesus taught about that topic or what James and Peter said about it. You would have a better grasp of the truth. Several of the tools you just read about can help you study the Bible this way.

When you study a passage, read it from several translations and compare them. For instance, in "God's Word for Today" from 2 Timothy 2:15, you probably realized that I gave the verse in two translations. Did you notice that the King James Version gave an emphasis to *studying* and the Holman CSB used *teaching* rather than *dividing*? Translations can increase your understanding.

Use center-column references, chain references, or a concordance to read other Scriptures using the same word or related to the same topic. One Bible gives references for "word of truth" in 2 Timothy 2:15 as "(Eph. 1:13, Jas. 1:18)."

② Read Ephesians 1:13 and James 1:18 in the margin and underline "word of truth" in each. What is the common topic in these two verses?

_____

Both of these verses focus on the role of the "word of truth" in our salvation or new birth. Use tools like these to study the Bible itself to better understand it.

STUDY WORDS IN THE BIBLE
In James 1:18 in the margin the term *firstfruits** is used. As you read the definition from the *Holman Bible Dictionary* in the margin, you learn that it can refer not only to the first crops harvested and dedicated to God but also to believers who were some of the first ones who came to Christ in a spiritual harvest. In James 1:18 the latter definition is the meaning used. *Strong's Dictionary* adds that this word comes from a compound of two other words meaning "the (Jewish) first-fruit (figuratively)." Word studies enrich your understanding of the Bible.

STUDY PASSAGES AND BIBLE BOOKS
Use a study Bible or a commentary to study a passage like the Sermon on the Mount (Matthew 5–7) or a whole Bible book like Matthew. These tools will help you understand the historical and biblical context for what was written. They can also help you understand passages in which various interpretations may be equally valid and worthy of consideration. If you were going to teach or preach on a topic, you would probably want to read a variety of commentaries on the text to assist your understanding and help you make life applications.

JOIN A BIBLE STUDY GROUP
You can study the Bible to great profit all alone. But God created the body of Christ (the church) so that we can help one another in Christian living. Studying the Bible with other believers can deeply enrich your own understanding and application of the Scriptures.

③ Read the list of Bible study options in the margin. Circle one you participate in or one that you know your church offers to members.

Pray and ask the Lord to guide you in your Bible study and to encourage you to study the Bible diligently so that you will have no reason to be ashamed.

Ephesians 1:13
"In Him you also, when you heard the word of truth, the gospel of your salvation— in Him when you believed— were sealed with the promised Holy Spirit."

James 1:18, NIV
"He chose to give us birth through the word of truth, that we might be a kind of firstfruits of all he created."

 Firstfruits: "The choice examples of a crop harvested first and dedicated to God. ... The Holy Spirit is spoken of as a 'firstfruits' (Romans 8:23), and believers are also spoken of as 'a kind of firstfruits' (James 1:18)."

_____

Larry Walker, *Holman Bible Dictionary* (Nashville: Holman Bible Publishers, 1991), 493.

Group Bible Study Options
• Sunday School class
• Home cell group
• Pastor's Bible class
• Weekday women's or men's Bible study
• Discipleship group
• Growth group
• Support group
• Other?

Day 5 • Doing God's Word

 Read and briefly meditate on "God's Word for Today" in the margin and respond to the Lord in prayer. Use the written prayer or pray your own.

God didn't give His Word just so that we could gain knowledge or win religious arguments. He wants to guide our daily living. As Creator, He knows exactly the way we need to live our lives in order to experience life at its best. Because He loves us, He wants us to experience His best.

Jesus set an example for us as One who chose to obey His Father's will. Jesus perfectly completed the work the Father gave Him to do. He humbled Himself and obeyed His Father even to the point of death on the cross (see Philippians 2:5-11).

1. Read the following statements of Jesus about the Father's will. Choose one that expresses your desire and add it to your Scripture-memory list. Write the verse on a card or on a separate piece of paper and start committing it to memory.

"I do not seek My own will, but the will of Him who sent Me" (John 5:30).

"My food is to do the will of Him who sent Me and to finish His work"(John 4:34).

"If you keep My commands you will remain in My love, just as I have kept My Father's commands and remain in His love" (John 15:10).

"'I have come to do Your will, O God.'" (Hebrews 10:7, NIV).

My favorite is the last verse. Jesus was quoting from Psalm 40:8. I've memorized that verse as a prayer to the Lord: "I desire to do your will, O my God; your law is within my heart" (NIV). The more we abide in Christ, the more we desire to please Him and obey Him. Then when obedience may be costly, we can pray like Jesus, "Not My will, but Yours, be done" (Luke 22:42).

 Pause to pray. Tell God of your desire to do His will. Pray back to the Lord the verse you chose above.

OBEDIENCE: A SOLID FOUNDATION FOR LIFE

Jesus told a parable about a wise and a foolish builder.

② Turn in your Bible to Matthew 7:21-27 and read about these two builders. What did the wise builder do with God's Word that the foolish builder did not do? Check one.

○ a. He heard God's Word but didn't bother to apply it in His life.

○ b. He built his house on a rock by hearing and doing God's Word.

③ What difference did it make when the storms of life came?

_____

_____

④ In the picture frames in the margin, draw one picture to illustrate the life (house) of one who hears God's Word and obeys it. Draw a second picture to illustrate the life (house) of one who does not live by God's Word.

When you choose to live your life according to God's design revealed in His Word, you will be better prepared to stand strong when the trials and problems of life come your way. Those who choose to disregard God's Word endanger themselves. They set themselves up for a fall when the problems of life come.

⑤ Suppose a close family member did something that very deeply hurt you. You allow it to affect your relationship. Bitterness begins to set in and keep the two of you apart. Then you read God's Word: "Bear with each other and forgive whatever grievances you may have against one another. Forgive as the Lord forgave you" (Colossians 3:13, NIV). Your Bible references Matthew 6:14-15, which reads, "If you forgive people their wrongdoing, your Heavenly Father will forgive you as well. But if you don't forgive people, your Father will not forgive your wrongdoing." What would you have to do to be a doer of the Word and not a hearer only?

_____

_____

 Close this week's study in prayer. Tell the Lord how much you want to do His will. Tell Him in advance that when He speaks to you through His Word, you will obey Him.

The Wise Builder

The Foolish Builder

Matthew 7:21

"Not everyone who says to Me, 'Lord, Lord!' will enter the kingdom of heaven, but only the one who does the will of My Father in heaven."

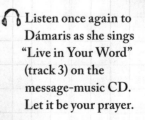 Listen once again to Dámaris as she sings "Live in Your Word" (track 3) on the message-music CD. Let it be your prayer.

43

Week 4 • **Pray in Faith**

"All the things you pray and ask for—
believe that you have received them,
and you will have them" (Mark 11:24).

Pray in Faith

Experience intimate communion with God. Receive God's counsel and directions, respond in praise and worship, receive cleansing through confession, and work together with God through petition for yourself and intercession for others.

Prayer is not just a religious activity; it describes a relationship with a person. Jesus spent time in prayer with His Father. Prayer was an important part of His decision making as He sought the Father's will and words. Jesus taught His disciples to be persons of prayer.

OVERVIEW OF WEEK 4

Day 1: Learning to Pray
Day 2: Responding to God in Prayer
Day 3: Asking in Prayer
Day 4: Giving God a Reason to Answer
Day 5: Praying Together

VERSE TO MEMORIZE

"All the things you pray and ask for—believe that you have received them, and you will have them" (Mark 11:24).

MESSAGE-MUSIC CD

"The Victory Is Won Through Prayer" (track 4)

DISCIPLESHIP HELPS FOR WEEK 4

"Suggestions for Praying Together" (p. 96)

WHY THIS WEEK WILL BE MEANINGFUL TO YOU

You will understand how to pray in faith and show your confidence in God by doing such things as …

- telling about a time you experienced God's wonders in answer to a specific prayer;
- responding to God's holiness, attributes, glory, and riches through confession, praise, worship, and thanksgiving;
- praying for yourself and others in response to God's invitation for you to ask;
- asking God to meet another person's needs according to His nature and character;
- removing from your life attitudes or actions that might hinder your prayers;
- praying in agreement with other believers for God's will to be done.

God's Word for Today

"He was praying in a certain place, and when He finished, one of His disciples said to Him, 'Lord, teach us to pray, just as John also taught his disciples.'" Luke 11:1

Responding to the Lord

Jesus, prayer is a relatively new thing for me. I've got much to learn. But I'll be a good student! Teach me just as You taught Your first disciples. Amen.

Optional Reading

Matthew 6:9-13 (below)

Matthew 6:9-13

"Our Father in heaven,
Your name be honored as holy.
Your kingdom come.
Your will be done
on earth as it is in heaven.
Give us today our daily bread.
And forgive us our debts,
as we also have forgiven
   our debtors.
And do not bring us into
   temptation,
but deliver us from the evil
   one.
For Yours is the kingdom
   and the power
and the glory forever. Amen."

Day 1 • Learning to Pray

Read "God's Word for Today" in the margin and respond to the Lord in prayer. As your time permits, consider the "Optional Reading" also. This week all of the "Optional Readings" are prayers. You may want to mark them in your Bible so that you can use them in your own prayer times. Today's reading is the Lord's Prayer (some call it the Model Prayer).

1) **Faith is an important aspect of prayer. Use your memory card and the tips on page 92 to begin memorizing Mark 11:24. Review your other verses.**

Prayer is not just a religious ritual in which you recite words that you hope might make a difference in your life. Prayer is a conversation with your Heavenly Father—the Creator and Ruler of the universe. When you pray, you talk to the One who made you. You spend time with the One who is your Master and who has all authority and power to will and do whatever He pleases. You can talk to Him as a child talks to a Father. At other times you talk to Him as a servant talks to a Master.

2) **Which of the following is an accurate definition of prayer? Check one.**
   ○ a. Words I memorize and regularly recite as a ritual I practice.
   ○ b. A personal pep talk I use to pump myself up and get myself into a positive frame of mind.
   ○ c. A relationship with my Heavenly Father—my Lord and Master— in which He speaks to me and guides me and I speak to Him.

Did you check the last definition? That's it! Prayer is communion with God. Though I want to teach you some things about prayer that may be helpful, you will best learn prayer by spending time with God in prayer and in His Word. Last week you learned about living in His Word. God speaks through His Word, so prayer and Scripture go together. You also will learn about prayer as you observe people in the Bible who prayed and read their prayers.

T. W. Hunt has been my mentor in regard to prayer. I worked with him as the editor of *Disciple's Prayer Life* and the coauthor of *In God's Presence* (now *Pray in Faith*). This week I'll share a number of things he has taught me about prayer.

3) **Read "10 Reasons to Pray" in the right margin. Circle three reasons you would like to learn to pray more effectively.**

🎧 As you read the words below, listen to Dámaris sing "The Victory Is Won Through Prayer" (track 4) on the message-music CD.

For the husband who has yet to choose the road of faith
For the child who's far from home, whose heart's been led astray
For the friend who's struggled long with what it means to believe
For every heartache, every trial — no matter what the need

Chorus
The victory is won through prayer / We will not be defeated or despair
The Lord of love is listening / Anytime and everywhere
The victory is won through prayer / The victory is won through prayer

In prayer we do battle and the faithful testify
Of the wonders they have seen the Savior do time after time
So let us press on pleading on behalf of those we love
He can do great things, so let us not give up
   Repeat chorus
What a privilege is ours to intercede / We stand the tallest on our knees
   Repeat chorus

④ If you can testify to a time when you experienced God's wonders in answer to a specific prayer, briefly describe that time below.

_____

_____

⑤ What major prayer request would you ask your group to join you in praying? Check one or write your own below or in the margin.
○ a. My spouse "has yet to choose the road of faith."
○ b. My child is "far from home, whose heart's been led astray."
○ c. My friend is struggling with "what it means to believe."
○ d. I have a heartache or trial.
○ e. Other: _____

 Take time to thank God for the privilege of talking with Him in prayer. Share with Him your major request. Begin praying for your small-group members. Ask God to teach each of you how to pray effectively and with power. Recite your memory verse and then ask God to teach you how to pray in faith.

The Victory Is Won Through Prayer

Words and music by Steve Siler, Tony Wood, Scott Krippayne. © Copyright 2004 Fifty States Music (admin. by Word Music, LLC)/Word Music, LLC (ASCAP)/Row J, Seat 9 Songs/Chips and Salsa Songs (All rights for the U.S. admin. by New Spring)/New Spring (ASCAP). All rights reserved. Used by permission.

10 Reasons to Pray
1. To spend time with God—the One you love
2. To identify with God by becoming like Him
3. To identify with God by working together with Him
4. To gain strength to resist temptation
5. To be made right with God
6. To find forgiveness, mercy, and grace
7. To learn God's will
8. To offer sacrifices of praise and thanksgiving to God
9. To learn authority
10. To release God's power

From T. W. Hunt and Claude V. King, *Growing Disciples: Pray in Faith* (Nashville: LifeWay Press, 2007), 23. Used by permission.

Day 2 • Responding to God in Prayer

Read and briefly meditate on "God's Word for Today" in the margin and respond to the Lord in prayer. Use the written prayer or pray your own.

One valuable benefit of prayer is that you can identify with God and become more like Him. As you read the Scriptures, you come to know what God is like as He has revealed Himself. As you respond to what He is like in prayer, He can mold and shape you to become more and more like Him. T. W. Hunt describes these as responding prayers.

CONFESSION IS RESPONDING TO GOD'S HOLINESS

God is holy, pure, righteous, and separate from us. When we realize what He is like in holiness, we will see the sin in our lives that is not like God. The natural response of a loving follower to God's holiness is to confess our sin and turn away from it because it is not like Him. That's what God wants. He wants us to be holy because He is holy (see 1 Peter 1:16). When you respond to God's holiness in confession, you are agreeing with God about your sin with the desire to be forgiven, cleansed, and restored to right fellowship with God. David gives us an example of confession: "I have sinned greatly in what I've done. Now, LORD, because I've been very foolish, please take away your servant's guilt" (2 Samuel 24:10).

① **What is one kind of responding prayer? Fill in the blanks and then take a moment to reflect on God's holiness and respond in confession if needed.**

_____ is responding to God's _____.

The next three types of responding prayers often blend together as you pray. When you start praising, worshiping, and thanking the Lord, the words often flow together and bubble forth in a stream of prayer. But each type of prayer is a little different. So let's look at each one separately.

PRAISE IS RESPONDING TO GOD'S ATTRIBUTES

God has revealed many more attributes or characteristics about Himself than holiness. In praise you lift up God's attributes as being valuable and worthy. As you praise Him for who He is, you will begin to value those traits and want to make them your own. He is patient, slow to anger, and forgiving. As you praise God for these, He can mold and shape you to become more like Him.

God's Word for Today

*"Shout triumphantly to the
LORD, all the earth.
Serve the LORD with
gladness;
come before Him with
joyful songs."*
Psalm 100:1-2

Responding to the Lord

Hallelujah, praise the Lord! May You be exalted in all the earth. You are worthy, O Lord, to be worshiped and praised. I adore You. I thank You for Your goodness and kindness, for Your love and mercy. I praise You, Lord God Almighty! Amen.

Optional Reading

Pray Psalms 149 and 150.

Psalm 57:9-10

*"I will praise You, Lord,
among the peoples;
I will sing praises to You
among the nations.
For Your faithful love is
as high as the heavens;
Your faithfulness reaches
to the clouds."*

② Read Psalm 57:9-10 in the lower left margin and underline two attributes the psalmist used in praising God. Notice that this is a prayer. You can use Scriptures like this one to voice your own praise to God.

WORSHIP IS RESPONDING TO GOD'S GLORY

When God acts because of His attributes, He reveals His glory. For instance, God is creative (an attribute). But the heavens and earth show His glory. They are the evidence that God is creative. The word *worship* means *to kiss toward*. When you worship God, you express toward Him your reverence, awe, honor, love, and adoration. Here are some examples of prayers of worship:

- I love You, Lord, because You first loved me and died for me.
- The heavens and earth declare Your glory. I'm amazed at Your wisdom, power, and greatness revealed in what I see.
- Lord, when I read of the way You dealt with the sins of Israel and Judah, I tremble in awe of Your holiness and purity. Yet your justice is fair and right.

③ In the margin I've listed some attributes of God. Below that list are some biblical words used in praise and worship. Read through these two lists and then take five minutes to respond to God in praise and worship.

THANKSGIVING IS RESPONDING TO GOD'S RICHES

God is the giver of everything that is good and perfect. He lavishes His love and bounty on us spiritually and physically. We become partakers in His riches. Thanksgiving is a response of gratitude to God's activity in your life. His desire is for you to experience an abundant life. Even when "bad" things happen, we can give thanks knowing that God causes everything to work together for our good as He shapes us into the image of Christ (see Romans 8:28-29).

④ Match the type of prayer on the left with the aspect of God you respond to in that type of prayer. Write a letter beside the number.

___ 1. Confession   a. God's riches
___ 2. Praise   b. God's glory
___ 3. Worship   c. God's holiness
___ 4. Thanksgiving   d. God's attributes

(Answers: 1-c; 2-d; 3-b; 4-a)

 Close today's lesson in prayer. Think about God's holiness, attributes, glory, and riches and respond to him in confession, praise, worship, and thanksgiving. If you prefer, write your prayer on a separate paper or in a journal.

Attributes of God

able	almighty
all-knowing	all-powerful
all-present	awesome
beautiful	blameless
blessed	compassionate
enthroned	eternal
exalted	faithful
forgiving	gentle
glorious	good
gracious	holy
indescribable	invisible
jealous	just
kind	living
majestic	merciful
mighty	patient
peaceful	perfect
pure	slow to anger
spirit	strong

Biblical Words for Praise and Worship

praise	exalt
laud	exult
rejoice	worship
adore	ascribe
glorify	honor
magnify	bless
hallelujah (praise Yahweh)	
hosanna (save, we pray)	

Romans 8:28-29
"All things work together for the good of those who love God: those who are called according to His purpose. For those He foreknew He also predestined to be conformed to the image of His Son."

Day 3 • Asking in Prayer

Read and briefly meditate on "God's Word for Today" in the margin and respond to the Lord in prayer. Use the written prayer or pray your own.

Jesus frequently invited and encouraged His followers to ask (see Matthew 7:7-8, 11; 21:22; John 14:13-14; 15:7,16; 16:23-26). He modeled asking for Himself and for others in His prayers.

① Your "Optional Reading" for today is a prayer of Jesus. Write below one or more requests Jesus made of the Father in this prayer.

_____

_____

Responding to the Lord

O Lord, I want to receive, find, and walk through Your opened doors. Give me perseverance to keep on asking, seeking, and knocking in prayer. Reveal Your will to me so that I can pray for Your kingdom to come and for Your will to be done on earth as it is in heaven. Develop me into a person of prayer. Amen.

PREPARING TO ASK

If you were invited to visit the king of a country, you would be given careful instructions about proper dress and behavior in the presence of royalty. When we pray, we need to give attention to preparing to enter the presence of the sovereign Ruler of the universe. We dare not just barge into His throne room. Wouldn't you want to have confidence that your request will be heard and answered? God has described for us conditions that lead to answered prayer.

② Read 1 John 3:21-22 below and underline words or phrases that describe the prerequisites for confidence in prayer.

Dear friends, if our hearts do not condemn us we have confidence before God, and can receive whatever we ask from Him because we keep His commands and do what is pleasing in His sight.

Optional Reading

John 17

Keeping God's commands and doing what pleases Him are important prerequisites to answered prayer. Scripture also describes things that hinder prayer, such as sin or iniquity (Psalm 66:18), anger and wrath (1 Timothy 2:8), broken relationships (Matthew 5:23-24; 1 Peter 3:7), doubting and unbelief (James 1:5-8), hypocrisy (Matthew 6:5), idolatry (Ezekiel 14:3), indifference to need (Proverbs 21:13), and unforgiveness (Matthew 6:14-15).

Take a moment to pray and ask God if He sees anything in your life that would hinder your prayers. Read the previous paragraph again, and if

God identifies something, confess your sin and turn from it. Ask God to forgive and restore you to right fellowship with Him.

PETITION AND INTERCESSION

Asking prayers can be divided into two types. Petition is prayer in which you ask for yourself or your family or group. Intercession is prayer in which you ask God to act in behalf of others. Both types are biblical prayers.

③ Read *and pray* the prayers in the right margin. Write a *P* beside the petition prayers for self and an *I* beside the prayers of intercession for others.

In Scripture God has revealed much about Himself, His will, and His ways. The more our prayers line up with God's will, the more likely they are to be answered. As you begin to pray about a particular matter, you might ask yourself: *Based on Scripture, what is God's will in this matter?* Sometimes God's will in a matter is clear. For instance, Paul writes, "This is good, and it pleases God our Savior, who wants everyone to be saved and to come to the knowledge of the truth" (1 Timothy 2:3-4). Peter says, "The Lord … is patient with you, not wanting any to perish, but all to come to repentance" (2 Peter 3:9). From these Scriptures we know God's will for the repentance and salvation of all people. You can pray for a person's salvation knowing that it is God's will. Similarly, you need not pray for God to help you do something He forbids in Scripture. That's one reason you need to live in the Word!

Practice asking for yourself and others. Select several items from the suggestions below and ask God to do His work in your life. Pray for one or two members of your small group as well. Check the ones you pray.

○ assurance	○ fullness of Spirit	○ patience
○ boldness	○ guidance, God's will	○ peace
○ Christian unity	○ healing	○ protection
○ conviction of sin	○ holiness	○ provision of needs
○ deliverance	○ hope	○ purity
○ endurance	○ humility	○ reconciliation
○ faith	○ integrity	○ spiritual fruit
○ faithfulness	○ justice	○ understanding
○ forgiveness	○ mercy	○ wisdom

Others: _____

_____

P = prayer of **Petition**
I = prayer of **Intercession**

"Search me, God, and know
my heart;
test me and know
my concerns.
See if there is any offensive
way in me;
lead me in the everlasting way."
Psalm 139:23-24 ____

"We are asking that you may
be filled with the knowledge
of His will in all wisdom and
spiritual understanding, so
that you may walk worthy of
the Lord, fully pleasing to
Him, bearing fruit in every
good work and growing in the
knowledge of God. May you
be strengthened with all power,
according to His glorious
might, for all endurance and
patience, with joy giving
thanks to the Father, who has
enabled you to share in the
saints' inheritance in the light."
Colossians 1:9-12 ____

"Teach me Your way, LORD,
and I will live by Your truth.
Give me an undivided mind
to fear Your name."
Psalm 86:11 ____

"Reveal to me the way
I should go,
because I long for You."
Psalm 143:8 ____

Day 4 • Giving God a Reason to Answer

Responding to the Lord
In Your name? Lord Jesus, teach me to ask in Your name. Help me abide in You in such a way that I know Your heart and mind on the matters for which I pray. I too want the Father to receive glory through You and through me. I know You want to reveal Your glory to those around me. What do You want me to ask for today? Lord, be glorified in me. Amen.

Optional Reading
Pray Ephesians 3:14-21.

Read and briefly meditate on "God's Word for Today" in the margin and respond to the Lord in prayer. Use the written prayer or pray your own.

This lesson I learned from T. W. Hunt has shaped my prayer life more than any other. T. W. noticed that great pray-ers in the Bible often gave God a reason to answer their prayers. He taught me to pray in the following ways.

PRAY FOR GOD'S GLORY
In "God's Word for Today" in the margin, Jesus gives a reason for prayers to be answered: "so that the Father may be glorified in the Son" (John 14:13). You can pray that God will be glorified in or through your life or in the circumstances about which you pray. That will lead you to ask the question, How will God receive the greater glory? When you pray for God's glory, you are asking that He be revealed in such a way that people will respond to Him in worship. Jesus prayed for God's glory to be revealed: "Now My soul is troubled. What should I say—Father, save Me from this hour? But that is why I came to this hour. Father, glorify Your name!" (John 12:27-28).

Think about some ways you can bring glory to God through the way you live and follow Him. Then pray and ask God to guide and strengthen you to bring glory to Him so that others will worship the God who is at work in you.

PRAY FOR GOD'S HONOR
God is concerned about His reputation. He doesn't want His name, reputation, or integrity to be disgraced or profaned. You may pray for God to be honored or that His name and reputation would not be disgraced by the actions of His people. When God threatened to destroy all of Israel in the wilderness, Moses appealed to God to refrain for the sake of His honor and fame:

> If You kill this people with a single blow, the nations that have heard of Your fame will declare, "Since the LORD wasn't able to bring this people into the land He swore to give them, He has slaughtered them in the wilderness" (Numbers 14:15-16).

APPEAL TO GOD'S CHARACTER
We looked at many of God's attributes on page 49. You can appeal to God's character or His nature and ask Him to function accordingly. You may learn

about God as you read Scripture and then ask Him to act that way in a circumstance you are praying about. For instance, in Psalm 68:5 (in the margin) we learn that God is a Father to the fatherless. That might prompt you to pray for the AIDS orphans in Africa, "Lord, as Father to the fatherless, please provide protection, food, and shelter to the orphans in Uganda." You may also need to be sensitive to the fact that God works through the body of Christ to carry out His work in our world. He may ask you to be part of the answer to that prayer. What a privilege we have when we can be laborers together with God!

Moses appealed to God's character in Numbers 14:18-19. God is loving, patient, and forgiving. Moses asked Him to act consistently with His character by forgiving the sins of His people.

 Think about the needs of a family member, a person in your small group, or a fellow church member. Review the list of attributes in the margin on page 49 and identify one way this person's needs might be met by God's acting in line with His character. Then pray by appealing to God's character.

ACKNOWLEDGE GOD'S SOVEREIGNTY

God is the Ruler of the universe. He has supreme authority over all people and every ruler, government, and nation. You can ask God to exercise His sovereignty or to make known His supreme authority. King Hezekiah prayed that way, and God answered his prayer (see 2 Kings 19:15-16,19 in the margin).

① **Match the reason on the left with the prayer example on the right.**

    ____ 1. Glory

    a. God of all comfort, Sue is troubled and grieving over her father's death. Comfort her and make her aware of Your presence.

    ____ 2. Honor

    b. Now that Bill has trusted You for salvation, set him free from his drug addiction to reveal Your power to his friends.

    ____ 3. Character

    c. Convince those in our church who are fighting one another for influence and control that Jesus can be the only Head.

    ____ 4. Sovereignty

    d. Help our youth group keep themselves pure and holy on our mission trip so that we will not bring discredit to Your work here.

 Close with a prayer of thanksgiving to the God who invites you to ask.

Psalm 68:5
"A father of the fatherless
and a champion of widows
is God in His holy dwelling."

Numbers 14:18-19
"The LORD is slow to anger
and rich in faithful love,
forgiving wrongdoing and
rebellion. … Please pardon
the wrongdoing of this people
in keeping with the greatness
of Your faithful love."

2 Kings 19:15-16,19
"LORD God of Israel who is
enthroned above the cherubim,
You are God—You alone—of
all the kingdoms of the earth.
You made the heavens and the
earth. Listen closely, LORD,
and hear; open Your eyes,
LORD, and see; hear the words
that Sennacherib has sent to
mock the living God. Now,
LORD our God, please save us
from his hand so that all the
kingdoms of the earth
may know that You are the
LORD God—You alone."

(Answers: 1-b; 2-d; 3-a; 4-c)

God's Word for Today

"If two of you on earth agree about any matter that you pray for, it will be done for you by My Father in heaven. For where two or three are gathered together in My name, I am there among them.'
Matthew 18:19-20

Responding to the Lord

Lord, I thank You that I'm not alone but that I have brothers and sisters in Christ I can pray with. I'm thankful for my small group. Teach us how to pray together and in agreement so that we may know the reality of Your promise for answered prayer. Let us know Your presence in increasing ways. Amen.

Optional Reading

Context for the prayer: Acts 4
Pray Acts 4:24-30.

"When they had prayed, the place where they were assembled was shaken, and they were all filled with the Holy Spirit and began to speak God's message with boldness."
Acts 4:31

Day 5 • Praying Together

 Read and briefly meditate on "God's Word for Today" in the margin and respond to the Lord in prayer. Use the written prayer or pray your own.

I agreed to lead a study about prayer at my church. At the first session I explained to the group that we would learn how to pray using *Growing Disciples: Pray in Faith* (a book I wrote with T. W. Hunt). Then when we came together each week, we would practice what we had been learning by praying together. Based on previous experience, I asked how many in the group were afraid to pray aloud. Many of the 18 in the group raised their hands. I tried to put them at ease by explaining that (1) I would not single out anyone and call on him or her to pray, (2) I would not ask them to pray around the circle, and (3) I gave them permission not to pray aloud. But I said, "We are going to pray together."

Later, I divided the group into smaller groups and gave this assignment: one at a time, ask each person in your group, "How may we pray for you?" Then pray for each person's requests. I was trusting that someone in each group would be courageous enough to pray.

The first request I heard was this: "We just learned that my 16-year-old daughter is pregnant. We don't know what to do. Please pray for us." That group began to cry out to God for this sister in Christ. Other groups were just as transparent and needy. Before the prayer time was over, we were all in tears. The next week one member brought a case of tissues and passed the boxes around, knowing this group might need them. Another member explained how God had answered a prayer from the previous week. Our prayer times became deeply meaningful as we cried out to God for real needs. And I think everybody learned to pray aloud. We were learning to talk to our Heavenly Father about our brothers and sisters in Christ. What a privilege that is!

1. **If your small group asked you that question ("How may we pray for you?"), what would your top request for yourself be?**

_____

_____

I love to pray together with a group. We can experience a different measure of Jesus' presence when we get together for prayer that we cannot experience alone (see Matthew 18:20). I learn to pray more effectively when I hear others pray. As we pray about one matter at a time, we pray all around it. Our prayers seem to feed off one another as the Holy Spirit guides our praying according to His will. One person's faith in prayer encourages my faith. Another's prayer using Scripture may redirect me to pray in line with Scripture rather than following my own thinking or wishes. Then I've experienced that moment in group prayer when we all begin to sense that God has revealed exactly what He wants to do in the matter, and we ask Him to do that. This is what I believe Jesus meant when He promised, "If two of you on earth agree about any matter that you pray for, it will be done for you by My Father in heaven" (Matthew 18:19).

② **As you read the following paragraph, circle the things that could hinder our prayers of agreement.**

Praying in agreement is not just my agreeing with you about what you ask. You and I first need to be in agreement with God in our relationships with Him. We can't allow sin, unbelief, or wrong motives to corrupt our relationship and still expect God to hear and answer our prayers. We also need to be in agreement with one another. We can't allow pride or broken relationships to keep us from a right relationship with one another.

Hindrances to Praying in Agreement
- sin
- unbelief
- wrong motives
- pride
- broken relationships

According to Paul, "The Spirit also joins to help in our weakness, because we do not know what to pray for as we should, but the Spirit Himself intercedes for us" (Romans 8:26). We can agree with one another and with God that we don't know what to ask in the matter about which we are praying. Our desires and opinions are not nearly as important as God's. So when we pray, we seek to know God's desire about the matter. As we bring our prayer into agreement with His plan, He stands ready to answer that prayer!

As we bring our prayer into agreement with His plan, He stands ready to answer that prayer!

③ **Which of the following is most important in prayers of agreement?**
○ a. We need to agree with one another.
○ b. We need to agree with God.

Our agreement with God is far more important than just agreeing with one another. We need to pray according to His will, not our own.

④ **Turn to page 96 and read "Suggestions for Praying Together."**
Underline the suggestions that seem particularly important to you.

Ask the Lord to teach you and your group to pray together effectively.

Listen once again to Dámaris as she sings "The Victory Is Won Through Prayer" (track 4) on the message-music CD.

Week 5 · **Fellowship with Believers**

"Let us be concerned about one another in order to promote love and good works, not staying away from our meetings, as some habitually do, but encouraging each other, and all the more as you see the day drawing near" (Hebrews 10:24-25).

Fellowship with Believers

Spend time with other believers, helping one another grow strong in the Lord and serving together to accomplish His kingdom purposes in the world.

When Jesus saved you, He placed you in the body of Christ with other believers. In relationship with other believers, you receive help to be all God wants you to be; and God uses you to contribute to meeting the needs of the rest of the body. Together we grow strong in our faith, and we accomplish the kingdom work of Christ in the world for which He died.

OVERVIEW OF WEEK 5
Day 1: Forgiving One Another
Day 2: Experiencing Fellowship
Day 3: Accepting One Another
Day 4: Loving One Another
Day 5: Keeping the Unity of the Spirit

VERSE TO MEMORIZE
"Let us be concerned about one another in order to promote love and good works, not staying away from our meetings, as some habitually do, but encouraging each other, and all the more as you see the day drawing near" (Hebrews 10:24-25).

MESSAGE-MUSIC CD
"I Choose Grace" (track 5)

DISCIPLESHIP HELPS FOR WEEK 5
"Guidelines for Reconciling and Forgiving" (pp. 97–98)

WHY THIS WEEK WILL BE MEANINGFUL TO YOU
You will understand how to fellowship with other believers and show your dedication to the body of Christ by doing such things as …
- forgiving those who have offended you and reconciling with those you have offended;
- encouraging others to love and do good works;
- loving others by meeting needs;
- regularly meeting with other believers in a setting where you can know, love, and care for one another;
- humbling yourself to get rid of pride.

Day 1 • Forgiving One Another

. . . .

↕ Read and meditate on "God's Word for Today" in the margin and respond to the Lord in prayer. As your time permits, consider the "Optional Reading" also. This week's "Optional Readings" give instructions for how we are to live and function in the body of Christ—the church. As you read the "Optional Reading" in your Bible, you may want to pause and talk to God about what you are reading. Cultivate your fellowship with Him.

God's Word for Today

"God's chosen ones, holy and loved, put on heartfelt compassion, kindness, humility, gentleness, and patience, accepting one another and forgiving one another if anyone has a complaint against another. Just as the Lord has forgiven you, so also you must forgive." Colossians 3:12–13

Responding to the Lord

Oh, Lord. Your commands seem to get harder all the time. Do You know how deeply people have hurt me? I guess You do. I need to tell You that I can't do this in my own strength. I need supernatural strength to forgive. Lord Jesus, You could forgive those who nailed You to a cross. You are in me. Would You enable me to forgive as You do? That is the only way I can obey, but I choose today to forgive because You have commanded it. Help me do it. Amen.

Optional Reading

Matthew 18:21-35

Right relationships are essential for a follower of Jesus Christ. Jesus has modeled for us how we should respond in relationships with others. Did you notice in "God's Word for Today" that Jesus has given us the model for forgiveness? You must forgive "just as the Lord has forgiven you." The truth is that you cannot forgive serious offenses without the help of the Holy Spirit. Forgiveness is not in our human nature. But God has commanded us to forgive for our own sake and for the way we represent Christ to others by forgiving. What He commands, He can help us obey.

I was leading a series of services in a church where I met a man who was saying things and acting in ways that were very unlike Christ. He was mean-spirited, harsh, cruel, and judgmental. He had offended many in his church. One night I prayed with him and asked if he had ever been hurt by anything that he had never gotten over. He immediately responded, "Yes." When he was 15, his father mercilessly beat him for something for which he had been falsely accused. He said, "I never forgave my dad for what he did to me." Now probably 40 years later his father was dead, and this man was very bitter.

I guided him to forgive his dad, and I prayed that his Heavenly Father would heal his wounded spirit. I had been teaching about forgiveness and reconciliation during the week. The next evening this man gave his testimony, and I saw a miracle of God's grace. He was gentle, humble, and repentant toward those he had offended. Bitterness can imprison you, but forgiveness can set you free.

① Have you ever been offended by someone in a way that makes it difficult for you to forgive that person, even to this day? ○ Yes ○ No

🎧 This week's song focuses on an action that is critical to right relationships—forgiveness. As you read the words on page 59, listen to Dámaris sing "I Choose Grace" (track 5) on the message-music CD.

Careless words cut so deep / A friend I trusted wounded me
For a while I held it in / I didn't see the bitterness as sin
I <u>lost</u> <u>hope</u> / I lost sleep / I lost the peace of Christ in me
All the hurt over time / Became a prison of my own design
The Holy Spirit made it clear I needed to let go
And let forgiveness flow, so

Chorus
I choose grace / I choose grace / I won't hold on to anger
To judge is not my place / I choose grace / I choose grace
When I look into my Savior's face / I choose grace

Maybe you've done the same / Cradled pride and nursed the blame
Now you see what it costs / All the loneliness, the life you've lost
If you've reached the point where you can't take another day
He can take the pain away, say
    Repeat chorus
Righting wrong relationships / Til hearts are in accord
Reconciled and restored, for
    Repeat chorus

I Choose Grace

Words and music by Steve Siler, Tony Wood, Scott Krippayne. © Copyright 2004 Fifty States Music (admin. by Word Music, LLC)/Word Music, LLC (ASCAP)/Row J, Seat 9 Songs/Chips and Salsa Songs (All rights for the U.S. admin. by New Spring)/New Spring (ASCAP). All rights reserved. Used by permission.

② Read the lyrics again and underline words or phrases that describe the possible consequences of holding on to bitterness or unforgiveness. I've underlined one for you.

③ Can you recall a time when you chose grace and forgiveness and experienced the release and joy of restored relationships? If so, briefly describe what happened.

_____

_____

④ Turn to page 97 and read the guidelines for reconciliation and forgiveness. Underline guidelines that will help you obey Christ in your relationships.

 Pray and ask the Lord to reveal to you any relationship in which you are holding on to bitterness or unforgiveness. Ask the Lord to enable you to choose grace and forgiveness. If you have more than one person or situation, make a list. Start choosing to forgive today. If you need to ask for forgiveness, be reconciled! Ask God to deliver you from these prisons.

Bitterness
can imprison you,
but forgiveness
can set you free.

God's Word for Today

"They devoted themselves to the apostles' teaching and to the fellowship, to the breaking of bread and to prayer. Everyone was filled with awe. And the Lord added to their number daily those who were being saved." Acts 2:42-43,47, NIV

Responding to the Lord

Lord, the early church sounds like a wonderful group. I'd like to be filled with awe and see people saved every day. Please show me how to fellowship with believers in my church in a way that will bear fruit for You. Amen.

Optional Reading

1 John 3

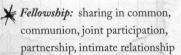 *Fellowship:* sharing in common, communion, joint participation, partnership, intimate relationship

1 John 1:3, NIV

"We proclaim to you what we have seen and heard, so that you also may have fellowship with us. And our fellowship is with the Father and with his Son, Jesus Christ."

Day 2 • Experiencing Fellowship

Read and briefly meditate on "God's Word for Today" in the margin and respond to the Lord in prayer. Use the written prayer or pray your own.

Many years ago, I shared with a discipleship group my frustration at my lack of discipline to get up early in the morning for a quiet time of Bible reading and prayer to start my day. After class Robert Carlton asked, "How can I help you?" After discussion we came up with a plan. We agreed to call each other six days a week (and take Saturdays off). Robert would call me at 5:00 a.m. on Monday, Wednesday, and Friday to make sure I was up for my quiet time with the Lord. I would call him at the same time on Tuesday, Thursday, and Sunday. If the person expecting the call had not received it by 5:05 a.m., he would call the other to make sure he was up. I never had to call Robert to wake him up, but Robert had to call me a number of times. The result? For several years I had a regular quiet time with God because Robert helped. I'm so thankful for a brother in Christ who was willing to spur me on to love and good deeds.

1. Hebrews 10:24-25 says we help one another by encouraging love and good works. Use your memory card and the tips on page 92 to begin memorizing these verses. Review your verses from previous weeks.

2. In what way could you use encouragement toward love and good deeds? Check a way or write your own.
   - a. I need encouragement to spend daily time in God's Word and prayer.
   - b. I need to be more faithful in meeting with other believers.
   - c. I need to become an active witness for Christ.
   - d. I want to show more compassion for others by serving and giving.
   - e. Other: _____

This week our focus is on our need to fellowship* with other believers. This fellowship is not just a social time with refreshments. This discipline describes a sharing of life at the deepest levels of personal and spiritual interaction. The model for our fellowship is the life we can come to share deeply with the Father and Jesus Christ His Son (1 John 1:3). When we have a right relationship with God, we can share that same intimate partnership with the rest of the body of Christ. John wrote:

If we say, "We have fellowship with Him," and walk in darkness, we are lying and are not practicing the truth. But if we walk in the light as He Himself is in the light, we have fellowship with one another, and the blood of Jesus His Son cleanses us from all sin (1 John 1:6-7).

(3) **Which of the following is the better definition of *fellowship?* Check one.**
○ a. A social time after church when we have snacks and chitchat.
○ b. A close and deep sharing of life and partnership with other believers.

To fellowship with believers, we share a partnership with others in the body of Christ in which we love and care for one another and experience God working in and through us to accomplish His kingdom purposes.

(4) **Let's look a little more closely at the first church in Acts to see how they experienced this fellowship. Turn in your Bible to Acts 2 and answer these questions.**
1. In verse 42 what four things were these believers devoted to?

_____

2. In verses 44-45 what did they do to help meet the needs of others?

_____

3. In verse 46 what two places did the disciples gather for meetings?

_____

These early disciples met daily in the temple courts and in their homes. They gathered for large-group worship and small-group fellowship. They didn't hesitate to share what they had to meet the needs of others. "No one said that any of his possessions was his own, but instead they held everything in common. There was not a needy person among them" (Acts 4:32,34). Can you imagine a church where love for one another ran that deep? Or one where there were *no* needy persons? The love the disciples shared with one another is part of what made Christ's message so attractive and fruitful. They devoted themselves to learning from the apostles, spending time together in fellowship, eating meals together, and praying together. What a church!

Pray for the fellowship of believers in your church. Ask God to develop in you and your group this kind of love and devotion.

They gathered for large-group worship and small-group fellowship.

Day 3 • Accepting One Another

. . . .

Read and briefly meditate on "God's Word for Today" in the margin and respond to the Lord in prayer. Use the written prayer or pray your own.

Paul wrote to the church in Rome and told them to accept one another just as Christ had accepted them. This lack of natural human prejudices would bring glory to God. Humans have a tendency to be prejudiced toward those who are different. A quick review of conflicts around the globe tells the story that people who are different often hate one another and fight and kill one another. Even Christians have a tainted record, but that should not be true.

Responding to the Lord
How blessed I am that You have accepted me, Lord. I certainly was not worthy of being accepted by You. I know it was all because of grace. But this is a hard saying. I must accept others in the way You've accepted me. Increase my faith, Lord. Give me Your heart of compassion and mercy so that I can overlook the outward things and love and accept people, because that makes me like You. I want to be like Christ. Help me, Lord. Amen.

① Take an honest look at your own thoughts about people who are different even though they may be Christians. Check below the people groups you struggle accepting in the same way Christ accepted you. People …

○ with a different skin color   ○ from a different country
○ who are poor and needy   ○ who are illiterate
○ who are rich   ○ who are well educated
○ from a different denomination   ○ with disabilities
○ who are much older   ○ who are Republicans
○ who are much younger   ○ who are Democrats
○ who are blue-collar workers   ○ who are managers/owners
○ Are there others? _____

Optional Reading
Romans 14:1–15:7

Jesus was criticized for being a friend of tax collectors and sinners. He set an example for accepting people that many others would not have accepted. For instance, He accepted:
• a Canaanite woman with a demon-possessed daughter (Matthew 15:21-28);
• a man with leprosy (Matthew 8:1-4);
• a Roman soldier (centurion) who had a sick servant (Luke 7:1-10);
• Nicodemus, a religious leader who sought Jesus but was too afraid to be seen with Him in the daylight (John 3:1-21);
• Peter, after he had denied Jesus three times (Mark 14:66-72; John 21:15-19);
• the Samaritan woman at the well who had been married five times and was living in adultery (John 4);
• the woman caught in the act of adultery (John 8:1-11);
• Thomas, even after he had doubted the resurrection (John 20:24-29);
• Zacchaeus—the hated tax collector (Luke 19:1-10).

When God was prepared to take the gospel to the Gentile (non-Jewish) world, He had to change Peter's thinking. He instructed Peter, "What God has made clean, you must not call common" (Acts 10:15). Then God sent Jewish Peter to the home of the Gentile Cornelius. Peter later explained, "I understand that God doesn't show favoritism, but in every nation the person who fears Him and does righteousness is acceptable to Him" (Acts 10:34-35). Those God accepts as sons and daughters we should accept also.

> "I understand that God doesn't show favoritism, but in every nation the person who fears Him and does righteousness is acceptable to Him."
> Acts 10:34-35

② **If you can think of a time when you were unjustly judgmental, critical, or unaccepting of another Christian, briefly describe that time.**

_____

_____

③ **If you have not already done so, read today's "Optional Reading." Then read the following list of instructions. Check any you realize God wants you to apply in a specific relationship that comes to mind.**
   - ○ a. Accept those from every nation, culture, and ethnic or social background who fear God and seek to do what's right and pleasing to Him (Acts 10:34).
   - ○ b. Accept those whose faith is weak (Romans 14:1).
   - ○ c. Don't pass judgment on others because of disputable matters (Romans 14:1).
   - ○ d. Don't look down on those who are more strict in their rules for living (Romans 14:3).
   - ○ e. Don't condemn those who are less strict in their rules for living (Romans 14:3).
   - ○ f. Don't stand in judgment or look down on those who are the Lord's servants and your brothers and sisters (Romans 14:4,10).
   - ○ g. Don't place any stumbling block in your brother's way or do anything in his presence that causes him to fall (Romans 14:13,20-21).
   - ○ h. Do what leads to peace and mutual edification (Romans 14:19).
   - ○ i. Don't cause others to stumble in their weak faith by practicing your liberty (Romans 14:21).
   - ○ j. Keep disputable matters between you and the Lord (Romans 14:22).
   - ○ k. Stand alongside and help those who are weak and fail (Romans 15:1).

Pray about the way you relate to other believers who may be different. Ask God to enable you to be just as accepting and loving toward others as He is. Pray about specific relationships that may need to be mended.

Day 4 • Loving One Another

Read and briefly meditate on "God's Word for Today" in the margin and respond to the Lord in prayer. Use the written prayer or pray your own.

God's Word for Today

"I give you a new commandment: love one another. Just as I have loved you, you must also love one another." John 13:34

"This is how we have come to know love: He laid down His life for us. We should also lay down our lives for our brothers." 1 John 3:16

Responding to the Lord

Well, Lord, the love part I like. I like to be loved by others, and that makes them easier to love. But I now realize You are talking about a depth of love I don't think I've ever known. Draw me ever nearer to You and the love You have shown me through Your death. Fill me up with Your Spirit of love and allow it to flow through me. Let me be a channel of Your love to splash all over others around me. Amen.

Optional Reading

1 Corinthians 13

Answers: 1-love, 2-choice, 3-fruit

I have a friend whose wife was diagnosed with Lou Gehrig's Disease. As she gradually lost control of her muscle functions, her church surrounded her and her family with loving service. Members took care of the yard work to allow my friend maximum time with his wife. Others helped with the children and household needs. In the latter days of her life, people were helping almost around the clock. At her funeral her pastor (of this relatively new church) posed the question "I wonder why God has given our young church this opportunity to love so deeply?" He and I discussed this afterward. We concluded that God was expanding the capacity of this church to love deeply so that He now could use the members to show a similar love to a lost world that needs Christ.

Genuine love is a distinguishing mark of those who have chosen to follow Christ. Jesus said, "All people will know that you are My disciples, if you have love for one another" (John 13:35). Christlike love seeks the welfare of others, but it is not based on the worthiness of the person loved. It comes from within the one who does the loving. Feelings are not the motivation for this love either. This kind of love is a choice you make. You choose to love. You choose to obey Christ's command to love one another. That love is a fruit of the Holy Spirit who lives in you. You become a channel of God's love flowing through you.

1. **In each statement below, circle one of the two words in parentheses to make the statement true.**
    1. People will know we are Jesus' disciples by our (faith / love).
    2. Christlike love is motivated by my (choice / feelings).
    3. Love is a (gift / fruit) of the Holy Spirit's work in me.

God loved the world and sent His Son to pay the penalty for our sin. Jesus showed us the full extent of His love when He laid down His life for us on the cross. That is how we know what love is. In "God's Word for Today" you read from 1 John 3:16 that we in turn should lay down our lives for our brothers. That is a hard saying to choose to live by, isn't it? Some people lay down their lives for others. But most of us will not be required to give up our physical lives for another. Stop and think, however, about some of things you might lay down because you love your brothers and sisters in Christ.

THINGS YOU CAN LAY DOWN IN LOVE

- material possessions
- money
- time to serve others
- position
- resistance to change

- your preferences
- your rights
- your expectations
- your opinion
- your pride

- dreams or ambitions
- goals or desires
- comfort or security
- reputation
- opposition to a project

② The Scriptures have much to say about what love is and what love is not. Read these verses and write in the margin a list of characteristics of what love is and what love is not. We'll discuss your lists in your next session.

Love Is …

"Love is patient, love is kind. It does not envy, it does not boast, it is not proud. It is not rude, it is not self-seeking, it is not easily angered, it keeps no record of wrongs. Love does not delight in evil but rejoices with the truth. It always protects, always trusts, always hopes, always perseveres" (1 Corinthians 13:4-7, NIV).

"Love must be without hypocrisy. Detest evil; cling to what is good. Show family affection to one another with brotherly love. Outdo one another in showing honor. Share with the saints in their needs; pursue hospitality" (Romans 12:9-10,13).

Love Is Not …

"You are called to freedom, brothers; only don't use this freedom as an opportunity for the flesh, but serve one another through love. For the entire law is fulfilled in one statement: 'You shall love your neighbor as yourself.' But if you bite and devour one another, watch out, or you will be consumed by one another" (Galatians 5:13-15).

③ Look back over the two lists. Circle a word or phrase in the "Love Is" list that you would like to improve on in your relationships with others. Circle a word or phrase in the "Love Is Not" list that describes a way you have acted in an unloving way toward another person.

④ Can you think of a time when you were the recipient of Christian love from a brother or sister in Christ in a way that was very meaningful? If so, briefly describe it in the margin.

Pray that God would so fill you with His Holy Spirit that love would naturally flow from your life to others. Ask for His forgiveness for the times you have acted in unloving ways. Choose today to love others.

God's Word for Today

"I, therefore, the prisoner in the Lord, urge you to walk worthy of the calling you have received, with all humility and gentleness, with patience, accepting one another in love, diligently keeping the unity of the Spirit with the peace that binds us." Ephesians 4:1–3

Responding to the Lord

Father, my world is filled with conflict. People just don't get along with one another very well. I'm afraid that is true in the church as well. But I see that it doesn't have to be so. Your Spirit binds us with peace into a unity we are to keep. Restore the unity in my church and family that will reflect well on You. Help me walk worthy of the calling I've received from You. Grant me humility, gentleness, patience, and love. Make us one in union with You. Amen.

Optional Reading

Colossians 3:1–4:1

John 17:23, NIV

"May they be brought to complete unity to let the world know that you sent me"

Day 5 • Keeping the Unity of the Spirit

⬍ Read and briefly meditate on "God's Word for Today" in the margin and respond to the Lord in prayer. Use the written prayer or pray your own. I'm going to ask you to read the "Optional Reading" later today.

I spoke to a group of about five hundred Asian-American pastors meeting in the annual convention of their denomination. Before the convention one leader said I needed to understand that they had bad tempers. On the side one of the men explained that for three years their guest speaker didn't get to speak because the business meeting went too long. They got into such heated debate over their business that they had no time left for the message.

I spoke from John 17 and Ephesians 2–4 about the direct connection between unity and spiritual awakening. Jesus said that our unity is the way a lost world will know He is God's Son: "My prayer is … that all of them may be one, Father, just as you are in me and I am in you. May they also be in us so that the world may believe that you have sent me" (John 17:20-21, NIV). Paul commanded us to "make every effort to keep the unity of the Spirit through the bond of peace" (Ephesians 4:3, NIV). The Holy Spirit brought great conviction because they lacked that kind of unity.

① **Read Jesus' prayer in John 17:23 in the margin below and circle the trait of His disciples that will convince the world that He is God's Son.**

Next I spoke about the body of Christ as a place where we experience the unity Christ provides. In the body of Christ there is only one Head—Christ. That means that our opinions don't matter. Only one opinion matters, and that is the opinion of the Head. Christ is Lord of the church. I explained that when they came to business meetings, they should have one mind and heart to say, "Lord, we don't have any will of our own. We want to know Your will."

Then I addressed the problem of their tempers. I pointed out that a fruit of the Spirit is self-control (Galatians 5:22-23). An out-of-control temper is sin and an evidence that the Spirit is not in control. Then we turned to Romans 6, and I showed them that they have "died to sin" and been set free from the slavery to sin. They didn't have to have a bad temper. They could be set free from it.

The next week I received a report. They said, "We started our business meeting the next day. We had such a spirit of unity that we finished in half a day, and we spent the other half of the day praying for one another. Many said it was our most spiritual meeting in our 16-year history." Christ can establish unity in His body! When He does, there is great joy, love, power, and peace.

② Read "God's Word for Today" again and underline the attitudes or character traits that would contribute to maintaining unity in the body.

Pride is probably the greatest barrier to unity in a body. When people think more highly of themselves than they ought, they conclude that their opinions must certainly be the best. They compete for control. They often criticize others and try to undermine their influence. They may act and believe that they don't need others, and the body of Christ is fractured. In Ephesians 4:1-2 Paul urged Christians to live worthy of their calling with "all humility." Humility is one attitude that contributes to unity. Gentleness, patience, acceptance, and love help maintain the unity of the Spirit as well.

③ Write a *P* beside the attitudes or actions below that come from pride and write an *H* beside the attitudes or actions that reflect humility.

___ boastful	___ cooperative	___ demanding
___ wants to be served	___ argumentative	___ selfish
___ willing to serve	___ impatient	___ selfless
___ submissive	___ patient	___ courteous
___ controlling	___ acts anonymously	___ rude
___ confesses sin	___ wants credit	___ prejudiced
___ covers up sin	___ encouraging	___ judgmental

④ Check your answers in the margin (right). If someone who knows you well used these two lists to evaluate your character as either proud or humble, which would he or she choose? Circle one: proud   humble

⑤ Turn in your Bible to Colossians 3:1–4:1 and read today's "Optional Reading." You may mark through "optional" today! List in the margin above several rules for living that would contribute to unity in a church.

Pray that the Holy Spirit will firmly establish a spirit of unity in your church. Confess any sin you have become aware of during today's study and ask for the Lord's forgiveness. Ask the Lord to guide and enable you to live in humility with gentleness, patience, acceptance, and love toward others in the body of Christ.

Answers: pride=boastful, wants to be served, controlling, covers up sin, argumentative, impatient, wants credit, demanding, selfish, rude, prejudiced, judgmental

humility=willing to serve, submissive, confesses sin, cooperative, patient, acts anonymously, encouraging, selfless, courteous

Listen once again to Dámaris as she sings "I Choose Grace" (track 5) on the message-music CD.

Week 6 · **Witness to the World**

"You will receive power when the Holy Spirit has come upon you, and you will be My witnesses in Jerusalem, in all Judea and Samaria, and to the ends of the earth" (Acts 1:8).

Witness to the World

Show and tell others what great things Christ has done for you. Together with the rest of the body of Christ, make disciples of Christ, beginning in your own world and going to the ends of the earth.

Jesus came with an assignment: to seek and to save those who are lost. He went to the cross so that a lost world could be reconciled (brought into a right relationship) with God the Father. He has given to us the ministry and message of this reconciliation so that others can experience a saving relationship with God. We have both the privilege and the responsibility to witness about Christ to the lost and dying world around us.

OVERVIEW OF WEEK 6

Day 1: Obeying the Final Command
Day 2: Surveying and Praying
Day 3: Cultivating Relationships
Day 4: Telling Your Story
Day 5: Introducing Jesus Christ

VERSE TO MEMORIZE

"You will receive power when the Holy Spirit has come upon you, and you will be My witnesses in Jerusalem, in all Judea and Samaria, and to the ends of the earth" (Acts 1:8).

MESSAGE-MUSIC CD

"Witness to the World" (track 6)

DISCIPLESHIP HELPS FOR WEEK 6

"Telling the Story of Jesus" (p. 99)

WHY THIS WEEK WILL BE MEANINGFUL TO YOU

You will understand how to witness to the world, and you will show your love for Christ and the world He loved and for which He died by doing such things as ...

- surveying your circles of relationships and praying for those who are yet to believe in Christ;
- reconciling and cultivating relationships with those who are yet to believe;
- showing God's love and mercy by meeting needs and forgiving;
- telling your story of the good things Jesus has done for you;
- introducing someone to Jesus Christ and what He has done for him or her;
- participating in a short-term mission trip.

Day 1 • Obeying the Final Command

Read and meditate on "God's Word for Today" in the margin and respond to the Lord in prayer. As your time permits, consider the "Optional Readings" also. The "Optional Readings" this week give you examples of those who were witnesses to their world. As you read them in your Bible, you may want to pause and talk to God about what you are reading. Cultivate your relationship with Him. Learn from the examples of others.

God's Word for Today

"Jesus came near and said to them, 'All authority has been given to Me in heaven and on earth. Go, therefore, and make disciples of all nations, baptizing them in the name of the Father and of the Son and of the Holy Spirit, teaching them to observe everything I have commanded you. And remember, I am with you always, to the end of the age.'"
Matthew 28:18–20

After Jesus rose from the grave, He spent 40 days with His disciples giving them last-minute instructions for their future service to His kingdom. At different times and in different ways, Jesus gave His followers a final command. The most familiar statement of the final command is in "God's Word for Today": "Go, therefore, and make disciples of all nations" (Matthew 28:19). In Mark 16:15 He said, "Go into all the world and preach the gospel to the whole creation." Another statement in Luke 24:47 reads, "Repentance for forgiveness of sins would be proclaimed in His name to all the nations." And John quoted Jesus as saying, "As the Father has sent Me, I also send you" (John 20:21). Earlier Jesus had described His assignment: "to seek and to save the lost" (Luke 19:10). His assignment for His followers is that we take the good news about His saving grace to those who need to know Him.

If I asked you where you were on September 11, 2001, when you heard that terrorists had attacked New York City and Washington, D.C., you would most likely be able to describe the experience in detail. When history-changing events like that take place, the experience gets etched into your memory in a way you don't forget.

Responding to the Lord

Lord, I'm so glad that someone obeyed Your command so that I could hear the good news about salvation. I'm thankful too for those who are teaching me to obey everything You've commanded. I'm learning! Now it's my turn. Teach me this week how I can be a faithful witness and tell others about what You've done for me. Use me to help others come to know You. Lead me to those You want to win. Amen.

Jesus carefully crafted His final words to His disciples. He knew that He would ascend into heaven before their eyes and that they would remember this day forever. He wanted to make sure they never forgot this critical assignment: "You will be My witnesses in Jerusalem, in all Judea and Samaria, and to the ends of the earth" (Acts 1:8). The future of His kingdom depended on their obedience to this assignment. For His work today He's depending on us!

① Jesus' final words to His disciples are recorded in Acts 1:8. Use your memory card and the tips on page 92 to begin memorizing these final words of our Lord. Pray that He will teach you and enable you to be His witness to your world. Review your memory verses from previous weeks.

Optional Reading
Acts 8

🎧 As you read the words below, listen to Dámaris sing "Witness to the World" (track 6) on the message-music CD.

Jesus' love is a holy fire / Burning in my soul
My heart beats with one desire / To make His salvation known

Chorus
I will be a witness to the world / Sharing the good news of all He's done
Living out the gospel with each breath / I will be a witness
A witness to the world

When we're bearing the fruit of grace / God is glorified
And knowing someone can be saved / I can't help but testify
   Repeat chorus
It's only by the Holy Spirit's power / That I can speak these words of life
To a world that is hurting and hungry
For the freedom that is only found in Christ
   Repeat chorus

② **Can you make these affirmations yourself? Check the ones with which you can agree.**
   ○ a. "Jesus' love is … burning in my soul."
   ○ b. I "desire to make His salvation known."
   ○ c. "I will be a witness to the world."
   ○ d. "Knowing that someone can be saved / I can't help but testify."

③ **Perhaps you are not able to make these affirmations yet. Describe your desire or willingness by checking a response or writing your own.**
   ○ a. I am willing, and I want to be a witness for Jesus Christ.
   ○ b. I am still *not* willing to obey the Lord's final command.
   ○ c. I will ask the Lord to give me the desire to obey His final command.
   ○ d. Other:_____

_____

↕ Pray that God will continue His work in your life in such a way that you will have a meaningful testimony of what He can do in a life. Ask Him to give you a deep love for those who do not yet know Christ. Ask the Lord to so fill you with His Holy Spirit that you will have all the power necessary to be a bold and fruitful witness for Jesus Christ.

Witness to the World

He wanted to make sure they never forgot this critical assignment: "You will be My witnesses in Jerusalem, in all Judea and Samaria, and to the ends of the earth" (Acts 1:8). The future of His kingdom depended on their obedience.

Day 2 • Surveying and Praying

Read and briefly meditate on "God's Word for Today" in the margin and respond to the Lord in prayer. Use the written prayer or pray your own.

① Quote your Scripture-memory verse, Acts 1:8.
What does the Holy Spirit provide for those who are witnesses?

_____

Yesterday you learned that Jesus wants you to be His witness. A witness* is one who testifies to what he has seen, experienced, or knows to be true.

② Do you qualify to be a witness for Jesus Christ? Do you know Him?
Have you experienced Him? Check your response or write your own.
○ a. Yes, I have personal experience of His saving grace.
○ b. No, I know only what others have told me. I don't have any firsthand experience with Christ.
○ c. Other: _____

SURVEYING YOUR CIRCLES OF INFLUENCE

If you have experienced the saving work of Jesus Christ in your life, you are qualified to be His witness. You can tell your story! The most natural people to tell your story to are those in your circles of relationships. Those who know what you were like before you came to Christ will notice the difference as you grow to be more like Him. Most frequently, these are also the people you would like to see come to faith in Christ.

③ Start making a list of people you know who do not yet believe in Jesus Christ as their Savior. Write a name or two in each circle of relationship listed below. You may want to start writing these names in a notebook.

A. Family or relative: _____

B. Friend or neighbor: _____

C. Coworker or acquaintance: _____

_____

God's Word for Today

"I am sending you what My Father promised. As for you, stay in the city until you are empowered from on high."
Luke 24:49

Responding to the Lord

Lord, I need to be "empowered from on high" too. I need the fullness and power of Your Holy Spirit to be at work in me to be a powerful witness. Teach me to be clean and dead to sin so that I can be filled up with You. Give me this power. Let Your Spirit overflow from my life to touch those around me with Your love and mercy. Amen.

Optional Reading

Acts 10

* **Witness:** one who testifies to what he has seen, experienced, or knows to be true

In *Concentric Circles of Concern* Oscar Thompson told the story of a friend who started making a list of people in his circles of influence. Dick had a great-aunt named Alice who lived in a nursing home in Oklahoma. He started praying for her, sent her a birthday card, and eventually visited her with his wife. Great-Aunt Alice began asking questions about what he was doing. As he began telling his story, he told her about the importance of his relationship with Jesus Christ. Though she had been a member of a church for most of her 82 years, no one had ever told her how she could have a personal relationship with Christ. She had never experienced a personal, saving relationship with Him before. That day she prayed and asked Jesus for forgiveness and salvation.

Months later Aunt Alice went to be with the Lord. Dick asked, "Dr. Thompson, what if I had not listed her in my concentric circles? What if I had not done my survey?"[1] That's why I want you to start surveying your circles of influence. God may want to work through your witness to bring them to faith in His Son.

PRAYING FOR THOSE YET TO BELIEVE

Now that you have a list of a few people in your circles of influence, you can start praying that they will come to faith in Christ.

(4) **Which person in your circles of influence would you most like to see come to faith in Christ? Write his or her name below.**

_____

(5) **Read below and in the margin the suggested ways to pray for those yet to believe. Check a few you think would be meaningful to pray. Lord, …**
- ○ Bring conviction of sin. Allow the consequences of his sin to cause him to desire a different life. Let him become fed up with his life as it is.
- ○ Bring her to understand the truth of her condition without Christ and to understand what Christ has done for her salvation.
- ○ Bring godly people into his life that will influence him for Christ.
- ○ Create circumstances that generate a need; then show your love by meeting needs through me or some others of your people.
- ○ Create opportunities for her to hear a witness for Christ from several different trusted sources. Use the timing and diversity of these witnesses to convince her that You are the Author behind them all.

Now use these ideas to pray for the person you listed above. As your time permits, start praying for others in your circles of influence.

Praying for Those Yet to Believe

- ○ Bring her to recognize her emptiness and purposelessness in life. Bring her to the end of herself so that she will turn to You.
- ○ Jesus, reveal the Father.
- ○ Father, exalt Jesus in his eyes and draw him to Jesus.
- ○ Prepare her life to receive the planting of Your Word.
- ○ Cause him to recognize his need for the Savior.
- ○ Prepare circumstances in his relationships through which a Christian (me if you choose) will have the opportunity to forgive him and thus reveal what Your mercy is like.
- ○ Bring her under the hearing and influence of Your Word through teaching or preaching. Create in her an openness to listen.
- ○ Reveal to me the time and way for me to share a witness about You and to tell him about the good news of salvation.
- ○ Lord, do whatever it takes to cause her to seek You.

1. W. Oscar Thompson, Carolyn Thompson Ritzmann, and Claude V. King, *Concentric Circles of Concern* (Nashville: Broadman & Holman, 1999), 100–101.

Day 3 • Cultivating Relationships

God's Word for Today

"Although I am free from all people, I have made myself a slave to all, in order to win more people. To the Jews I became like a Jew, to win Jews; to those under the law, like one under the law—though I myself am not under the law— to win those under the law. To those who are outside the law, like one outside the law—not being outside God's law, but under the law of Christ— to win those outside the law. To the weak I became weak, in order to win the weak. I have become all things to all people, so that I may by all means save some."
1 Corinthians 9:19–22

Responding to the Lord

Father, so many people around me do not have a saving relationship with Your Son. I so want them to know You. Use me as Your instrument to cultivate relationships through which You can draw them to Jesus. I'm available. Amen.

Optional Reading
Luke 19:1-10

Read and briefly meditate on "God's Word for Today" in the margin and respond to the Lord in prayer. Use the written prayer or pray your own.

In the parable of the sower (Luke 8:5-15) Jesus described a hundredfold productivity of seed (the Word of God) that is sown on good soil (people with honest and good hearts). But the seed that fell on the hard path, in rocky places, or among the thorns was unproductive. When a farmer cultivates a field, he plows the hard soil and removes the rocks and weeds so the soil will be ready to receive the seed he plants. In spiritual matters it is lives that must be prepared to receive God's Word and the message of salvation.

Jesus frequently demonstrated this approach as he fed and healed people to gain access to their responsive hearts. In today's "Optional Reading" Jesus went to Zacchaeus's house even though people were critical of His being the guest of a sinful tax collector. By cultivating a relationship with Zacchaeus, Jesus brought salvation to his household that day.

 Based on 1 Corinthians 9:19-22 ("God's Word for Today"), why did Paul, the writer of 1 Corinthians, make himself "a slave to all"?

_____

Paul cultivated relationships with people through his service to them so that he could win more people to saving faith in Christ. By spending time with people, you show an interest in their lives. By meeting the needs of people, you show Christ's love to them. By forgiving them, you show them what God's mercy is like. By cultivating relationships with the people in your circles of relationship, you will help prepare them to respond to your witness.

A CHURCH SHOWS GOD'S LOVE AND MERCY
Some years ago, a pastor in Arkansas related the following story of what had taken place in his church during the past six months. A young couple from a nonchurch background came to faith in Christ. Soon after their conversion their car was stolen. The pastor encouraged them to begin praying for the person who stole their car, knowing that the person probably needed Christ.

A month later, a 15-year-old boy was arrested for the crime. This couple went to visit him in jail, but their excitement to finally meet this boy caught him a bit off guard. They showed an interest in him and in his family. They discovered that his mother was in the hospital, so they went to visit her as well.

Because of financial problems the woman had lost their home. When the time came for her to be dismissed from the hospital, she would be homeless. This young couple took her to their own home to meet her needs and show the love of Christ. When the church learned of their actions, they decided to help. They secured an apartment for the woman and furnished it. Overwhelmed by the love of Christ demonstrated by this couple and the church, the woman trusted Christ as her Savior. Her son came to faith in Christ as well.

Not long after their conversions the woman's ex-husband was paroled from prison and came to town looking for his family. While in prison, he had become a Christian himself. After studying the Bible and taking Bible-correspondence courses, he sensed that God was calling him into vocational ministry. He came home in hopes that he could be reconciled with his wife. What joy this church experienced as they watched God reunite a family in such a miraculous way. Unselfish ministry to others can be a powerful testimony of the love of Christ through the body of Christ.

 As you read the following paragraphs, underline ways you can cultivate relationships with those in your circles of relationships who need Christ.

WAYS TO CULTIVATE RELATIONSHIPS

Reconcile broken relationships. If you have a broken relationship with a person who needs Christ, you need to do your part in getting the relationship right. If you have caused an offense, ask forgiveness and make restitution if necessary. If you've been offended, forgive the offender and act as though you've forgiven him.

Spend time with people. Get to know them and allow them to get to know you. Share meals individually or with your families. Participate in common interests, sports, or hobbies. Develop an interest in things that interest them. As your relationship develops, your witness will become more effective.

Show God's love by meeting needs. Watch for needs you can meet. Get others to help when the needs are greater. Allow God to love people through your deeds.

 Ask God to show you a way to cultivate your relationship with one of the people for whom you are praying. What do you need to do?

Unselfish ministry to others can be a powerful testimony of the love of Christ through the body of Christ.

Ways to Cultivate Relationships
1. Reconcile broken relationships.
2. Spend time with people.
3. Show God's love by meeting needs.

Week 6 » Day 3

75

God's Word for Today

"Go back home to your own people, and report to them how much the Lord has done for you and how He has had mercy on you." Mark 5:19

Responding to the Lord

Lord, I don't know how to answer all of the questions people may raise about You and Your Word. I know I can tell them, "I don't know the answer to that, but I'll find somebody who may be able to help." And I can tell people what You've done in my life; I've experienced it. That's my story. I am a witness to what You've done; I was there! Prepare the way and use me as I tell my family, relatives, neighbors, and coworkers about the good things You've done for me. I will be Your witness to my world! Amen.

Optional Reading

John 4:4-42

A genuine testimony of a recently changed life can be very powerful.

Day 4 • Telling Your Story

 Read and briefly meditate on "God's Word for Today" in the margin and respond to the Lord in prayer. Today's "Optional Reading" is a part of our lesson. Please read the story of the Samaritan woman in John 4:4-42. As you read, notice the impact this new believer had on her city.

When the Samaritan woman learned that Jesus was the Christ (the Messiah), she couldn't wait to carry that good news to her town. She brought her town to meet Jesus Christ.

1. **When this woman became a witness of Christ, what difference did it make in the lives of the people in her town?**

_____

_____

2. **How long had she known Jesus before she became a witness for Him?**

_____

She had known Jesus for only moments when she became a witness for Him. She didn't attend a class or go to Bible college or seminary first. She just told what she knew and had experienced. As a result, "many of the Samaritans from that town believed in him because of the woman's testimony" (John 4:39, NIV). A genuine testimony of a recently changed life can be very powerful.

In Mark 5 we read about a man who was in bondage to demons and whose life was out of control. His family life had been destroyed. When Jesus healed him and set him free, everything changed. The man wanted to travel with Jesus, but Jesus gave him a special assignment: "Go back home to your own people, and report to them how much the Lord has done for you" (Mark 5:19).

Now that you have been saved and set free from sin, Jesus gives you the same assignment: to tell those who know you what great things He has done for you. Paul describes our assignment in 2 Corinthians 5:17-20 (see text in the margin on p. 77): "We are ambassadors for Christ." We have been changed, and now we have been given a ministry and a message of reconciliation. We have the privilege and responsibility of pleading with people to "be reconciled to God."

THE IMPORTANCE OF TELLING YOUR STORY

I was young when I first asked my dad to tell me how to become a Christian. He shared the good news with me, and soon I decided to repent of my sins and receive this free gift of eternal life. On the following Sunday morning I was playing with a friend before the worship service. I told him about the decision I had made, and he began to ask questions. We talked during much of the service, and he decided that he wanted to receive Christ as His Savior also. We both shared our decisions with the church that morning.

Years later, I received a call. This friend died while serving in the military. My dad and I stood by his casket with his mother and reflected about the decisions we had made that Sunday morning years before. I had no idea at the time how important telling my story about Jesus could be to the life and destiny of another.

③ Look back at your response to activity 4 on page 73. Suppose you learned that this person would soon be leaving this world and entering eternity without Christ. How would you respond? Check one or write your own.

○ a. I would immediately make plans to go tell him my story and introduce him to Jesus Christ.

○ b. I would give up hope of her ever coming to Christ.

○ c. I would pray that God would send someone else to share Christ with him.

○ d. Other: _____

④ What's your story? In the margin write notes in answer to the questions below to outline your story. You may want to write more details on a separate sheet.

What was your life like before you came to Christ?

What happened to cause you to recognize that you wanted and needed the Savior?

How did you become a Christian?

What changes for good have taken place since you trusted Christ and He gave you His Holy Spirit to live in you?

Pause to pray and thank God for the changes He has made in your life. Ask Him to give you the courage and boldness to tell others about Jesus and what He has done in your life.

2 Corinthians 5:17-20

"If anyone is in Christ, there is a new creation; old things have passed away, and look, new things have come. Now everything is from God, who reconciled us to Himself through Christ and gave us the ministry of reconciliation: that is, in Christ, God was reconciling the world to Himself, not counting their trespasses against them, and He has committed the message of reconciliation to us. Therefore, we are ambassadors for Christ; certain that God is appealing through us, we plead on Christ's behalf, 'Be reconciled to God.'"

Notes on My Story

God's Word for Today

"You will receive power when the Holy Spirit has come upon you, and you will be My witnesses in Jerusalem, in all Judea and Samaria, and to the ends of the earth."
Acts 1:8

Responding to the Lord

Power and confidence in Your presence in my life—that's what I need. Empty me of self and cleanse me of sin. Fill me with Your Holy Spirit. Then show me where You want me to go for You. I want the whole world to know You. Use me everywhere You choose. I will be a witness to the world! I will tell others my story about You. Amen.

Optional Reading

Acts 16:11-40

Day 5 • Introducing Jesus Christ

Read and briefly meditate on "God's Word for Today" in the margin and respond to the Lord in prayer. Use the written prayer or pray your own.

Witnessing to the world begins with naturally sharing your life with others and telling them your story of the difference Christ has made in your life. That witness is most effective when shared through a relationship you have in common. But seeing your life on display is not all they need. People also need to know Jesus Christ and what He has done for them through the cross. Let me suggest some ways you might share Jesus with them.

① **Read the following list and underline ways you would be willing to introduce Jesus Christ to others.**

1. Share your testimony and explain why and how you placed your faith in Jesus Christ and His redeeming work on the cross. You could add a summary of the good news and tell Jesus' story (see p. 99).
2. Invite a Christian friend to join your relationship—one who has experience sharing the plan of salvation with others. You share the live testimony.
3. Give to someone or read and explain to them a gospel tract like *Steps to Peace with God* or *How to Have a Full and Meaningful Life*.
4. Give to someone or read and explain a New Testament that has been marked with the plan of salvation like *Here's Hope New Testament*.
5. Join a group study that will teach you how to explain the gospel clearly, like FAITH Sunday School Evangelism Strategy or *Share Jesus Without Fear*.
6. Watch an evangelistic movie or a television program together and discuss it.
7. Offer a small-group study of a book like Serendipity House's *Knowing Jesus*.
8. Invite the person to a Sunday School class or a small-group Bible study that is open and sensitive to seekers who don't yet know the Lord.

Your church probably has tracts, marked New Testaments, or other resources you can use to introduce others to Jesus Christ. Check with your church, your pastor, or your local Christian bookstore for tools you can use.

② **Think about the people you have listed from your circles of influence who have not yet believed in Christ. To which of the above ways do you think they would be most responsive? # _____ Consider how you might use this method to introduce them to Christ.**

GOING TO THE ENDS OF THE EARTH

Notice in Acts 1:8 ("God's Word for Today") the progression His witnesses take: from their home in Jerusalem outward to all the world. Jerusalem was the home base from which the witnesses would go. Judea was the larger territory around Jerusalem, but it was primarily relatives (people from the same Jewish tribe). Going to Samaria meant crossing ethnic, racial, and religious barriers to be His witnesses. And the assignment included "the ends of the earth."

③ **Match the location on the left with the correct description on the right.**

___ 1. Jerusalem   a. People from a different race, ethnicity, or religious background

___ 2. Judea   b. Other countries of the world

___ 3. Samaria   c. Kinfolk or relatives by blood and by marriage

___ 4. Ends of the earth   d. Territory beyond hometown but nearby

                 e. Hometown, immediate family

(Answers: 1-e; 2-c, d; 3-a; 4-b)

One day "when [Jesus] saw the crowds, He felt compassion for them, because they were … like sheep without a shepherd" (Matthew 9:36). Because of His compassion Jesus said to His followers, "The harvest is abundant, but the workers are few. Therefore, pray to the Lord of the harvest to send out workers into His harvest" (Matthew 9:37-38). Evidently they prayed, and in the next verse we read that Jesus sent out the twelve apostles on a mission trip. Jesus looks out over your city and our world with that same compassion today.

Jesus calls us to be His witnesses. Everyone who has become a new creation in Jesus Christ is a witness of that personal experience. As we function as the body of Christ, each member has different gifts that he or she uses to specialize in additional ways in witnessing to the world. Some are gifted intercessors who pray with power to penetrate the darkness. Others demonstrate God's love through ministry evangelism. Others actively seek to persuade people to be reconciled with God. Some are gifted at training new Christians to be faithful disciples. And still others may go to distant places, either on short-term assignments or for life, to take the good news to the ends of the earth.

↕ Take a moment to pray that the Lord of the harvest will send out workers today in our world. As you pray, think of the desperate needs of the world without Christ. Think about the needs of your larger family, your city, and your nation. Then ask the Lord what part He wants you to play in that harvest. As He guides you, write a note in the margin.

> Everyone who has become a new creation in Jesus Christ is a witness of that personal experience.

🎧 Listen once again to Dámaris as she sings "Witness to the World" (track 6) on the message-music CD.

Week 7 · **Minister to Others**

"Serve one another through love"
(Galatians 5:13).

Minister to Others

Show God's love by meeting needs of others inside the body of Christ and those who are yet to believe. Build up the body of Christ through loving service in His name.

Jesus modeled a life of service for His disciples and for us. He did not come to be served but to serve others. His calling to us is to a life of service to those who are needy both in the body of Christ and in the world that has not yet believed. When we love and serve others who are needy, we show our love for Christ Himself, and God uses that service to build up the body of Christ.

OVERVIEW OF WEEK 7

Day 1: Serving like Jesus
Day 2: Serving to Build Up the Body of Christ
Day 3: Showing Love by Meeting Needs
Day 4: Comforting One Another
Day 5: Growing as a Disciple

VERSE TO MEMORIZE

"Serve one another through love" (Galatians 5:13).

MESSAGE-MUSIC CD

"Able" (track 7)

DISCIPLESHIP HELPS FOR WEEK 7

"Courses to Help You Grow in Discipleship" (p. 100)

WHY THIS WEEK WILL BE MEANINGFUL TO YOU

You will understand how to minister to others and show your love by doing such things as …
- accepting places of humble service, following Jesus' model;
- finding your place of service in the body and becoming equipped to serve there;
- showing God's love by meeting needs of people in the church and the world;
- showing your love for Christ by ministering to those in need;
- comforting others who face difficulties through which God has already helped and comforted you;
- praying on the spot for people who need your prayers;
- telling another believer about how God is growing and maturing you as a follower of Jesus Christ and encouraging him or her to grow with you;
- choosing to take next steps in growing as a disciple of Jesus Christ.

Day 1 • Serving like Jesus

God's Word for Today

"You know that those who are regarded as rulers of the Gentiles dominate them, and their men of high positions exercise power over them. But it must not be like that among you. On the contrary, whoever wants to become great among you must be your servant, and whoever wants to be first among you must be a slave to all. For even the Son of Man did not come to be served, but to serve, and to give His life—a ransom for many."
Mark 10:42–45

Responding to the Lord

Lord Jesus, You gave me a wonderful example of One who serves others. I'm so grateful to You for all You've done for me. I want to become a servant like You, knowing that servanthood is how You determine greatness in Your kingdom. Open my eyes to see needs of others; and give me the boldness, courage, and resources needed to serve them. Make me more and more like You. Amen.

Optional Reading

John 13:1-17

Read "God's Word for Today" in the margin and respond to the Lord in prayer. As your time permits, consider the "Optional Reading" also. As you read it in your Bible, mark verses that are particularly meaningful. Talk to God about what you are reading. The "Optional Readings" this week focus on instructions and examples of service. Today's "Optional Reading" describes how Jesus modeled service by washing the disciples' feet.

1. Our final week of study turns our attention to ministry to others. Use your memory card and the tips on page 92 to begin memorizing Galatians 5:13. Take time to review all seven memory verses. Have you memorized them all?
   ○ yes   ○ no   ○ a few of them   ○ most of them

One day James and John asked Jesus to give them special places of leadership in His kingdom. When the other disciples heard about it, they were upset with them. Jesus called the Twelve together and explained that importance in His kingdom would be measured on a different basis.

2. What are some ways humans typically claim greatness or influence? Check all that apply.
   ○ a. People claim influence based on their title or position.
   ○ b. People exercise influence because of their wealth or education.
   ○ c. People falsely assume power based on a presumed ethnic or racial superiority.
   ○ d. People claim places of influence because of cultural or social status.
   ○ e. People claim influence based on personal accomplishment or fame.

Did you check them all? You could have. People use all of these reasons to claim a position of influence or power over others. Jesus, however, gave a different basis for measuring greatness in His kingdom. The great ones in His kingdom are those who serve. Jesus went on to offer Himself as an example of sacrificial service. He said, "The Son of Man did not come to be served, but to serve, and to give His life—a ransom for many" (Mark 10:45). On the night before He went to the cross, He acted like a common slave and washed the dirty feet of His disciples. He said, "I have given you an example that you also should do just as I have done for you" (John 13:15). By Christ's standards a place of humble service in the body of Christ is an important place of greatness.

As you read the words below, listen to Dámaris sing "Able" (track 7) on the message-music CD. Underline how we are able to fulfill God's call.

It's such a big world we've been called to make a difference in
There are seeds to plant, hearts to change, and souls to win
There are lives to touch with a healing word
There is hope to share and when we serve

Chorus
We are able through the gifts of God / We are able by His Spirit
We must become less / He must become more
It's only when we're filled with the Lord / That we are able

We can reach out with this message in all confidence
Knowing that the Father finishes what He begins
And commissioned by the One we trust
With the Lord of all at work in us
    Repeat chorus
It doesn't matter if you think your talents are great or small
God doesn't call the equipped / He equips the called / So …
    Repeat chorus

③ Reflect on these encouraging words. Check the one or two statements that are most encouraging to you and explain why in the margin.
○ a. "We've been called to make a difference."
○ b. "We are able by the gifts of God."
○ c. "We are able by His Spirit."
○ d. "We can reach out … in all confidence."
○ e. "The Father finishes what He begins."
○ f. "The Lord of all at work in us."
○ g. "God … equips the called."
○ h. "We are able!"

④ Do you recall a time God called you and then equipped you to complete an assignment for Him? Or has God asked you to do something in ministry that you have not yet obeyed? If so, briefly describe one or both experiences in the margin.

Take a moment to thank God for what He has already done in your life to call and equip you. Pledge to carry out the assignments He has given.

Able

Words and music by Steve Siler, Tony Wood, Scott Krippayne.
© Copyright 2004 Fifty States Music (admin. by Word Music, LLC)/Word Music, LLC (ASCAP)/Row J, Seat 9 Songs/Chips and Salsa Songs (All rights for the U.S. admin. by New Spring)/New Spring (ASCAP). All rights reserved. Used by permission.

By Christ's standards a place of humble service in the body of Christ is an important place of greatness.

God's Word for Today

"It was he who gave some to be apostles, some to be prophets, some to be evangelists, and some to be pastors and teachers, to prepare God's people for works of service, so that the body of Christ may be built up until we all reach unity in the faith and in the knowledge of the Son of God and become mature, attaining to the whole measure of the fullness of Christ."
Ephesians 4:11-13, NIV

Responding to the Lord

Lord Jesus, I'm a part of the body of Christ for my world. This is a lofty goal that we should be built up in unity to become mature and reach fullness in Christ. I know only You could accomplish such a miracle. Thank you for giving me leaders who can train me and prepare me for service in such a way that I can contribute to building up Your body. Show me when and how to serve. Help me grow in maturity and Christlikeness, too. Amen.

Optional Reading

Ephesians 4

Day 2 • Serving to Build Up the Body of Christ

Read and briefly meditate on "God's Word for Today" in the margin and respond to the Lord in prayer. Use the written prayer or pray your own.

The more you become like Jesus, the more you will be a servant like Jesus. Together with other believers we make up the body of Christ, with Christ as our Head. Ephesians 4:11-13 explains how the body of Christ is built up, experiences unity, grows in spiritual maturity, and becomes increasingly Christlike.

① Read Ephesians 4:11-13 again. Match the people on the left with the correct function on the right. Write a letter beside each number.

___ 1. apostles   a. Equip God's people for service
___ 2. prophets   b. Prepare and serve the body of Christ to build it up.
___ 3. evangelists
___ 4. pastors/teachers
___ 5. the rest of God's people   *(Answers: 1-a; 2-a; 3-a; 4-a; 5-b)*

Is that the way you thought the church was to function? Too many churches think they pay a pastor or staff member to do the work of serving the church. But healthy churches function the way God intended them. Leaders equip God's people, who all have a part in building up the body of Christ and in growing into maturity and Christlikeness.

When I was working in New York City, I took a group of visiting seminary students to an ethnic church in Brooklyn for a Sunday service. We were escorted through the main worship center, where about 1,500 people met for a French service. In the gymnasium about 500 youth and young adults met for a service in English. After the service we met with Pastor Thomas. We learned that their church was active in world missions and aggressively started new churches in other cities (about 50 to date). One student asked, "How many paid staff members do you have?"

We were all shocked by his reply: "None." That's not your typical church these days, especially not one with 2,000 in worship on Sundays. He said, "JPMorgan Chase pays my pension."[1] He worked for the bank to earn a living. This church had started in his home almost 40 years earlier. He went on to explain his conviction that "when you get saved, you get a job. My job is to be the pastor." He asks his people to pray and seek the Lord's will about their job in the church. Then he and other leaders help equip them to share in the work God has assigned their church. Sounds like Ephesians 4:11-13, doesn't it?

② On the Disciple's Cross diagram on page 93, five types of ministry are listed. Look at the diagram and complete the following chart.

Discipline	Ministry
1. Live in the Word	Ministry of _____
2. Pray in Faith	Ministry of _____
3. Fellowship with Believers	Ministry of _____
4. Witness to the World	Ministry of _____
5. Both Fellowship and Witness	Ministry of Service

Pray and ask the Lord to reveal to you any ministry assignment He may have for you at this point in your Christian life. Keep in mind, however, that sometimes you need to be on the receiving end of a ministry. We don't put God on our timetable, so if He doesn't speak to you about a specific ministry assignment, you don't have to make one up.

③ Read in the margin the brief descriptions of these broad ministries. Write below anything you sense God wants you to do in ministry to others or describe a way you need to receive ministry from someone else.

Ministry for me to undertake: _____

_____

_____

_____

_____

_____

Ministry I need to receive: _____

_____

Being part of the body of Christ involves finding your place in service to the Lord. Ask the Lord to show you where you can begin serving Him and His church. Pray for your leaders as they lead your church to follow Christ as Head and to function as the body of Christ before a watching world.

Five Ministries of the Disciple's Cross

1. *Ministry of Teaching/ Preaching.* God calls some to teach and preach to help people understand and apply God's Word in their lives. You don't need a position to teach others what God is teaching you.

2. *Ministry of Worship/ Intercession.* Worship is individual and corporate ministry to the Lord. Intercession is serious prayer in behalf of others.

3. *Ministry of Nurture.* Believers need to grow from being new in faith to maturity. They need to learn to apply God's truths in relationships. They need a model to help them learn to be faithful followers of Jesus Christ.

4. *Ministry of Evangelism.* All should be witnesses, but some are especially gifted to lead others to faith in Christ in very productive ways.

5. *Ministry of Service* is meeting needs of believers and those who have not yet believed.

Week 7 » Day 2

---

1. Paid pastors and staff are biblically allowed. Pastor Thomas has chosen to follow the example of the Apostle Paul, who chose to preach the gospel free of charge. See 1 Corinthians 9:7-27.

85

Responding to the Lord

Father, You first loved me and sent Your Son to pay for my sins. Now You've saved me from sin and given me the wonderful assignment of being Your coworker in the kingdom. I'm blessed! Give me Your heart of compassion for those who are needy around me. Help me enjoy serving them through love. Amen.

Optional Reading

Matthew 25:31-46

Day 3 • Showing Love by Meeting Needs

Read and briefly meditate on "God's Word for Today" in the margin and respond to the Lord in prayer. Use the written prayer or pray your own.

In Matthew 25:31-46 (today's "Optional Reading") Jesus told a sobering story about the end times. In the end Jesus will separate His sheep from the goats. His sheep will enter eternal life, and the goats will go to eternal punishment.

1. If you haven't done so, read Matthew 25:31-46 in your Bible. Write beside the people described below what Jesus expected to be done for them.

1. Hungry: _____

2. Thirsty: _____

3. Stranger: _____

4. Naked: _____

5. Sick and prisoner: _____

Those who are His sheep will have served Christ and ministered to Him by feeding the hungry, quenching the thirst of the thirsty, showing hospitality to strangers, clothing the naked, and visiting the sick and imprisoned. Those who serve others in these ways have served Christ Himself. Jesus was not saying that eternal life could be earned in this way. Rather, He made clear that those who belonged to Him would care about the needy and have compassion on them just as Christ would. Jesus described ways you can show your love and care for Him by loving and meeting the needs of others.

In *Concentric Circles of Concern* Oscar Thompson told a story about one of his students. Jerry got off work one night and found that his motorcycle mirror had been stolen. He found it on another motorcycle in the company parking lot. In anger he took back his mirror and flooded the thief's motorcycle so that it wouldn't start. The next day Jerry began to feel guilt about his response. As he prayed, God led him to respond in love. That night Jerry bought a new mirror and put it on the other person's motorcycle. He left a message explaining that he was a Christian and that God wouldn't tolerate his kind of behavior. He asked forgiveness, signed his name, and gave a phone number. Later that night Jerry got a call. The thief explained that he'd stolen many things in his life, but no one had every treated him like this before. He wanted to talk. That night Jerry led the man to faith in Christ. In his book Thompson gives this definition of *love*: "Love is meeting needs."[1]

(2) **Suppose you knew people who had the needs listed in the left column below. How could you demonstrate your love by meeting those needs? Match each need on the left with a way to meet the need on the right.**

Need	Possible Way to Meet the Need
___ 1. Lonely	a. Find/provide shelter
___ 2. Grieving	b. Babysit the children
___ 3. Jobless	c. Spend time talking/visiting
___ 4. Hungry	d. Network him with an employer needing his skills
___ 5. Single parent	e. Teach literacy class or tutor
___ 6. Homeless	f. Provide food
___ 7. Can't read	g. Comfort, help her talk about good memories

Ways to meet a need may vary, depending on the circumstances. If God wants you to help meet the need, spend enough time with the needy person or group to see how to help effectively. Keep in mind that love will be costly and may require sacrifice. Sometimes you will be unable to meet the need alone. Don't hesitate to enlist others to help meet the need.

Prayer should also be a major part of your seeking directions on ways to help. Not every need is a call for your response. However, when you become aware of a need, ask, "Lord, do You want to meet that need through me?" Then obey Him.

You may minister to other believers in the body of Christ and show love by meeting needs. God has given us the church as a place to practice loving. He can use the needs in the church to expand your capacity to love deeply. But God will also bring across your path those who have not yet believed. They may be unlovely, mean, or even evil. As you love these who don't expect your love, God may work through you to bring them to faith in His Son.

 Pray about the people in your circles of contact. Are there needy people God is already prompting you to help? Ask Him. Pray that your church will be sensitive to the needs of people in your community.

"Love is meeting needs."

(Answers: 1-c; 2-g; 3-d; 4-f; 5-b; 6-a; 7-e)

When you become aware of a need, ask, "Lord, do You want to meet that need through me?" Then obey Him.

1. W. Oscar Thompson Jr., Carolyn Thompson Ritzmann, and Claude V. King, *Concentric Circles of Concern* (Nashville: Broadman & Holman Publishers, 1999), 149–152.

Day 4 • Comforting One Another

Read and briefly meditate on "God's Word for Today" in the margin and respond to the Lord in prayer. Use the written prayer or pray your own.

God's Word for Today

"Blessed be the God and Father of our Lord Jesus Christ, the Father of mercies and the God of all comfort. He comforts us in all our affliction, so that we may be able to comfort those who are in any kind of affliction, through the comfort we ourselves receive from God."
2 Corinthians 1:3-4

Responding to the Lord

God of all comfort, I thank You for the ways You comfort me when I need to be comforted—times when I've needed Your mercies. Now, because I've been comforted, I've been equipped to help others who are experiencing the same needs I had. Love them through me. Comfort them through me. Let Your love flow through me to touch the lives of others around me. Amen.

Optional Reading

Isaiah 58

Henry Blackaby and I were teaching *Experiencing God* at a conference in New Mexico. I was leading a time of testimonies when a young man from Texas asked for prayer. His father had just died. He asked if someone who had experienced the death of a father would come and pray with him. The man sitting beside him had prayed as he entered the room that evening, "Lord, where do You want me to sit?" He had felt led to sit beside this young man. Now he knew God was up to something. His father had died not long before, and God had comforted him during that time of grief. He knew how to pray for this brother who was grieving the loss of his dad because he had been in that same position himself.

After he prayed, they began to talk about their experiences. The man who prayed found out that the man from Texas lived in the very city where his widowed mother lived. The man who had requested prayer now realized God was inviting him to help the mother of the man who had just prayed for him. God places members in the body of Christ to show concern for other members. When one needs comfort, God uses other members to provide it.

God is the God of all comfort. He is the Father of mercies. "He comforts us in all our affliction, so that we may be able to comfort those who are in any kind of affliction, through the comfort we ourselves receive from God" (2 Corinthians 1:4). When you have experienced a trial or a difficult circumstance, and God has worked to bring you through the problem, you have been equipped for His service.

 Have you been comforted by God in a way that would equip you to minister to someone else in similar circumstances? If so, when and how did God comfort you? Consider experiences of abandonment, loneliness, the death of a loved one, a business failure, the loss of a job, a financial crisis, the illness of a family member, homelessness, deliverance from an addiction, being a victim of abuse or crime or a natural disaster, dealing with a wayward child, or any other experience in which God comforted you.

HELPING THE WEAK, OPPRESSED, AND NEEDY

In Isaiah 58 God describes activities that are pleasing to Him:

> To break the chains of wickedness,
> to untie the ropes of the yoke,
> to set the oppressed free,
> and to tear off every yoke?
> Is it not to share your bread with the hungry,
> to bring the poor and homeless into your house,
> to clothe the naked when you see him,
> and to not ignore your own flesh and blood?
> If you get rid of the yoke from those around you,
> the finger-pointing and malicious speaking,
> and if you offer yourself to the hungry,
> and satisfy the afflicted one (Isaiah 58:6-7,9-10).

God made wonderful promises to people who do such things. He promised light, recovery, righteousness, protection, and answered prayer. He promised to lead, provide for, and strengthen you.

 Pause to pray and ask God to reveal to you anyone to whom He wants you to minister. Invite Him to open your eyes in the coming days to reveal people who have needs that you can meet. Also consider that God may want you to work together with another person or group to accomplish ministry that you cannot do alone. Consider such things as …
- helping the poor, needy, hungry, homeless;
- helping widows or orphans (either here or in foreign lands);
- taking a stand for a person who is oppressed, mistreated, abused, or needing justice;
- helping a stranger or an alien;
- standing up for one who is persecuted, taken advantage of, cheated, robbed, discriminated against, or defrauded.

② **Write below any action you sense God is leading you to take.**

_____

_____

_____

When you have experienced a trial or a difficult circumstance, and God has worked to bring you through the problem, you have been equipped for His service.

Responding to the Lord

Lord, what a prayer Paul prayed for the Ephesians! I pray this for my church and especially for the people in my small group. Grow us. Strengthen us. Fill us up with the fullness of Christ. Amen.

Optional Reading

Colossians 1

Day 5 • Growing as a Disciple

Read and briefly meditate on "God's Word for Today" in the margin and respond to the Lord in prayer. Use the written prayer or pray your own.

When I was in elementary school, my family visited another family. They had a child who was probably seven years old, but he was still in diapers and had to be fed and carried around because of a disability. I remember being very disturbed. Children are supposed to grow up, not remain as babies. That's also true for disciples. God never intended for us to remain babies in Christ. He wants us to grow. I pray that the past seven weeks have helped you grow significantly in your walk of following Christ. This is not the end of your growth but just a time of transition. What is next for you?

1. If your leader has given you a spiritual-assessment tool, take time to complete it before continuing. If you don't have one, consider going online to *www.lifeway.com*. Download and print out the Spiritual Growth Assessment Tool. In a subjective way this tool helps you identify how well you are developing in the six disciplines we've studied. It's not scientific, but the results together with prayer may give you some direction about where you need to work in your continuing growth as a follower of Jesus Christ.

Pray and ask the Lord to guide you in choosing a next step in your discipleship training.

2. Turn to page 100 and read the recommendations for further study in each of the disciplines. Circle those that you believe would be particularly helpful in your next steps of spiritual growth. In your small-group session you will be able to discuss next steps with others.

REVIEWING *THE CALL TO FOLLOW CHRIST*

As we draw this study to a close, I'd like for you to review what God has been saying and doing in your life. Look back through the daily lessons and identify elements that have been particularly meaningful or helpful to you.

3. Which week of this study has been most meaningful and why?

_____

_____

④ Which of the Scripture-memory verses has been most meaningful to you and why? Circle it in the margin and explain why below.

_____

⑤ Which of the message-music songs has been the most meaningful to you and why? Circle it in the margin and explain why below.

_____

⑥ What activity (whether assigned or done on your own) have you done during this study that has been the most meaningful or practical in your growth in Christlikeness and why? Consider such things as …
• daily quiet time, a Bible study session, a time of prayer alone or with others;
• a walk with the Heavenly Father;
• an act of obedience or sacrificial service;
• deliverance from sin, an answer to prayer, or a reconciled relationship;
• teaching, witnessing to, or ministering to another person;
• giving or receiving comfort or ministry in the body of Christ.
• Other:

_____

_____

_____

_____

Take some time in prayer and reflect on what God has been teaching you the past seven weeks. Thank Him for the ways He has revealed Himself and for the ways He has helped you grow. Ask Him to enable you to become more like Christ in your thinking, in your attitudes, and in your actions. Ask Him to personally guide you as you seek to grow into full maturity in Christ. Give Him permission to work freely in your life.

Thanks for allowing me to share these weeks with you. Now may you "grow in the grace and knowledge of our Lord and Savior Jesus Christ. To Him be the glory both now and to the day of eternity. Amen" (2 Peter 3:18).

Scripture-Memory Verses
Luke 9:23
John 15:5
James 1:22
Mark 11:24
Hebrews 10:24-25
Acts 1:8
Galatians 5:13

Message Music
The Call
Moments with the Master
Live in Your Word
The Victory Is Won
    Through Prayer
I Choose Grace
Witness to the World
Able

Week 7 » Day 5

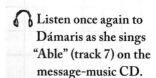 Listen once again to Dámaris as she sings "Able" (track 7) on the message-music CD.

Tips for Memorizing Scripture

1. Select verses for memorization that are particularly meaningful to you or that are related to a topic you are studying. As you read your Bible, mark verses you may want to memorize later. Select verses from your pastor's sermon or from a small-group Bible study. Or study a topic and make a list of verses that help you understand the topic.

2. Write the verse and reference on a card. On the reverse side write the reference only. If you have a computer, you can type or copy verses into a word-processing program and print them on perforated business cards. Use perforated index or postcards for longer passages. Write the date on the card for later reference.

Therefore being justified by faith, we have peace with God through our Lord Jesus Christ:

Justification
Peace

Romans 5:1

3/19/80

3. Seek understanding. Read the verse in its context (the verses before and after it, like a paragraph or even a chapter). Study the verse and try to understand what it means. If you have a concordance or dictionary of Bible words, you may want to read definitions or synonyms of words you don't understand. A commentary can help you understand other aspects of the verse's meaning.

4. Meditate and pray. Think about what the verse means to you. How would you apply the verse to your life? Ask God how He wants to apply the verse in your life. Does it teach you something about Him? Is it a command to obey or a sin to avoid? Is it a principle that should guide your actions or decisions? Does it describe a desirable character trait for you to develop or one for you to avoid? Is it a prayer to pray or a call to worship? What should be different in your life because of this truth?

5. Read the verse aloud several times.

6. Learn to quote the verse one phrase at a time. Divide the verse into short, meaningful phrases. Learn to quote the first phrase word for word. Then build on it by learning the second phrase. Continue until you are able to quote the entire verse word for word.

7. Recite the verse to another person. Invite him or her to check your memory or explain what God is teaching you through the verse.

8. Regularly review the memorized verse. During the first week or two, carry the card in your pocket or purse. Pull it out for review several times daily during waiting periods, like riding an elevator, sitting at a stoplight, during a coffee or lunch break, or waiting for an appointment. Review the verse at least daily for the first six weeks. Review it weekly for the next six weeks and monthly thereafter.

The Disciple's Cross

The Disciple's Cross diagram and teaching come from a discipleship course titled *MasterLife* by Avery T. Willis Jr. Hundreds of thousands of people around the world have grown as faithful followers of Jesus Christ by studying this course together. Many have become leaders, pastors, and missionaries as a result of this study. The Disciple's Cross illustrates the six disciplines in *The Call to Follow Christ*, which were originally taught in *MasterLife*. When you complete your study of *The Call to Follow Christ*, I highly recommend the four six-week courses in *MasterLife* as a valuable next step in your growth as a disciple.

MASTERLIFE RESOURCES

MasterLife 1: The Disciple's Cross (001116284)

MasterLife 2: The Disciple's Personality (001116285)

MasterLife 3: The Disciple's Victory (001116286)

MasterLife 4: The Disciple's Mission (001116287)

MasterLife Book Set (all four books): (001116322)

MasterLife Leader Guide (001116288)

MasterLife Leader Kit (005157084)

MasterLife: Developing a Rich and Personal Relationship with the Master (001069212)

To order, call (800) 458-2772, visit *www.lifeway.com*, or go to the LifeWay Christian Store serving your area.

Bible Study Tools

BIBLE TRANSLATIONS

Language usage changes over time. Modern translations of the Bible seek to take the original Hebrew and Greek texts and translate them in ways that clarify for readers the accurate meaning of the text. Because Greek and Hebrew words can be translated differently, depending on their contexts, reading the same passage in several different translations can add insight or understanding. (Note that paraphrases like *The Message* are different from translations. They may reflect the writer's personal interpretation or emphasis of the Scriptures by adding to the original text. They can be meaningful supplements to your study, but they are different from translations.) Commonly used translations:

• King James Version
• Holman Christian Standard Bible
• New International Version
• New American Standard Bible
• New King James Version

AUDIO BIBLE

Many Bible translations are available in audio or download formats for listening convenience.

CONCORDANCE

Many Bibles have a concordance at the back. That section lists words and the references to places where those words are used in the Bible. An exhaustive concordance lists every occurrence of the word. Computer or Web-based Bible study tools usually allow you to search for a word and give you the results you would find in a concordance. Using a concordance, you can find out what other Scriptures may have to say about that topic. The most commonly used concordance is *Strong's*

Exhaustive Concordance of the Bible. It not only lists all occurrences of a Bible word, but it also has a numbering system by which you can learn which Hebrew or Greek word is being used in a particular passage.

CENTER-COLUMN OR CHAIN REFERENCES

Some Bibles also list additional references to similar words or topics in a center column, in footnotes, or as a chain of references you can follow by moving from one Scripture referenced to another. For instance, if you look at 2 Timothy 2:15, the center-column reference might list Ephesians 1:13, Colossians 1:5, and James 1:18 as additional references to "word of truth."

> **An Approved Worker**
> 14 Remind them of these things, charging them before God[a] not to fight about words;[f] this is in no way profitable and leads to the ruin of the hearers. 15 Be diligent to present yourself approved to God, a worker who doesn't need to be ashamed, correctly teaching the word of truth.[g] 16 But

STUDY BIBLE

A study Bible includes tools in addition to the Scripture text to help you study your Bible. They typically include an introduction to each Bible book explaining the context of when and why it was written and by whom. They include notes for verses and topics to explain what is meant by the verse or to help you make personal application to your life. Study Bibles also have a variety of tools that can deeply enrich your Bible learning. For instance, one lists all of the prophecies about Jesus' second coming so that you can study that future event. Ask a teacher or your pastor to recommend a good study Bible if you need one.

BIBLE DICTIONARY

A Bible dictionary explains the meaning of Bible words, concepts, topics, people, history, and/or geography. An example is *Holman Illustrated Bible Dictionary*. Some dictionaries, like *Vine's Expository Dictionary of New Testament Words*, include only the meanings of Bible words.

BIBLE HANDBOOK

Handbooks provide background information about the Bible books and text in simple and compact form for introductory study.

WORD-STUDY TOOLS

These books give in-depth analysis of Greek and/or Hebrew words and describe their use in Scripture and in contemporary Greek and Hebrew texts from Bible times. Examples include:
• *Holman Treasury of Key Bible Words* by Eugene Carpenter and Philip Comfort
• *Word Pictures in the New Testament* by A. T. Robertson

COMMENTARY

Commentaries come as single volumes or whole series of books written to explain the texts in Scripture. They can help you gain a great depth of knowledge and insight from a passage or Bible book. Commentary authors are normally scholars who have carefully studied the Scriptures, and they write to help you understand the meaning and application of the Scriptures. Some commentaries are more devotional in nature; others are more academic. Examples of commentaries include:
• Matthew Henry's *An Exposition of the Old and New Testaments* (5 volumes)
• *Holman Concise Bible Commentary* (1 volume)

BIBLE ATLAS

Typically, a Bible atlas includes a list of Bible place names, maps, and photographs of modern Bible locations. Others add archaeological information on Bible sites. One such atlas is *Holman Bible Atlas*.

HARMONY OF THE GOSPELS

This tool takes the texts from the Gospels Matthew, Mark, Luke, and John and provides a chronological comparison of the texts for studying the life and teachings of Jesus Christ.

COMPUTER AND ONLINE BIBLE STUDY TOOLS

Many Web sites provide free online Bible study tools. These include a variety of Bible translations, concordances, dictionaries, commentaries, word-study tools, maps, and devotionals to aid your Bible study. Check out *http://bible.lifeway.com* for an example. Computer programs make available whole libraries of Bible study tools for more in-depth study. An example is *Bible Navigator*.

BIBLE STUDY BOOKS AND WORKBOOKS

Another tool that can be helpful to your study of the Bible is a Bible study book or workbook. In these an author has done much of the study in a variety of resources for you. He or she shares insights from this study. In a workbook the author then engages you through interactive questions and activities to gain understanding and to make application of the text or topic. Some studies are topical, while others focus on a specific Bible book or passage. Go to *www.lifeway.com* for other discipleship workbooks like this one.

Suggestions for Praying Together[1]

The following are suggestions for praying together in a group. They should not be seen as rigid rules but only as suggestions. Enjoy your times of corporate prayer.

1. Acknowledge God's presence and active participation with you in prayer.
2. Use common language rather than church words.
3. Speak for yourself, using *I, me, my,* or *mine* rather than *we, us, our,* or *ours* unless you know your prayer represents the group's thoughts on the matter.
4. Save your closings (like "Amen" and "In Jesus' name") until the end of the prayer time.
5. Prepare yourselves through prayers of confession, cleansing, and reconciliation.
6. Spend time in prayers of worship, praise, and thanksgiving.
7. Normally, spend the bulk of your time in prayers of petition and intercession. Share requests as you pray rather than spending time at the beginning to list and discuss requests.
8. Pray about one subject at a time.
9. Take turns praying about a subject. Continue on that subject as long as God seems to guide the praying.
10. Be specific in what you ask of God.
11. Ask the Holy Spirit to guide your praying according to God's will. Pay attention to the Holy Spirit's direction for praying.
12. Consider God's viewpoint and give God a reason to answer.
13. Use biblical prayers, principles, patterns, and promises to guide your requests. Pray the Scriptures.
14. Seek Spirit-guided agreement with others in your prayers.
15. Seek to put yourself in the place or mind-set of those for whom you are praying so that you can "feel" what they feel.
16. Listen to the prayers of others for direction or answers to your prayers.
17. Respond to the prayers of others.
18. Pray for one another. Ask: How may we pray for you? And then pray.
19. When time permits, pray until you sense God has finished leading your prayers.
20. Consider writing down the subjects for which you have prayed so that you can watch with anticipation for God's answers.
21. When God answers one of your prayers, remember to thank Him and watch for opportunities to testify to His wonderful work.

---

1. Adapted from T. W. Hunt and Claude V. King, *Growing Disciples: Pray in Faith* (Nashville: LifeWay Press, 2007), 110. Used by permission.

Guidelines for Reconciling and Forgiving[1]

IF YOU ARE THE OFFENDER

Jesus commanded those who have offended others, "If you are offering your gift on the altar, and there you remember that your brother has something against you, leave your gift there in front of the altar. First go and be reconciled with your brother, and then come and offer your gift" (Matthew 5:23-24).

Guidelines to reconcile with those you have offended:

1. Pray and ask God to help you have thorough and genuine repentance.
2. Go to the person to make things right in obedience to God.
3. Put the most difficult person first on your list.
4. Confess your sin to God and to those directly affected by the sin.
5. Don't apologize. Ask for forgiveness.
6. Go in person (best choice), call by phone (second choice), or write a letter (last resort).
7. Don't reflect negatively on the other person or his actions or attitudes. Deal only with your part of the offense.
8. Make restitution (pay for the offense) when appropriate.
9. Don't expect to receive a positive response every time. Continue to pray for and seek reconciliation with an unforgiving person. Jesus' command is "Be reconciled" (Matthew 5:24).

IF YOU ARE THE ONE OFFENDED

Forgiving someone who has offended us is often very difficult, even for Christians. Nevertheless, God's Word is very clear in defining our responsibility to forgive those who have hurt us:

1. Forgiveness is fully releasing another from the debt of the offense.
2. The person who forgives is the one who has to pay the price of forgiveness, just as Jesus paid the price for you on the cross.
3. You are never more like Jesus than when you forgive and show grace and mercy. Being offended provides you with the invitation to reveal Christ to the offender by your forgiveness.
4. Forgiveness does not mean that the offense was not wrong.
5. Forgiveness is not permission for the offender to do it again. It does not require you to place yourself in harm's way again.
6. Forgiveness does not mean that you will fully forget. However, you choose not to hold the offense against the person any longer.
7. How much do you forgive? Jesus said, "70 times seven" (Matthew 18:22). In other words, forgive an unlimited amount.
8. Jesus said, "If [your brother] sins against you seven times in a day, and comes back to you seven times, saying, 'I repent,' you must forgive him" (Luke 17:4). In other words, even if the offender really doesn't repent and change his ways, you should still forgive.
9. Even if the person doesn't believe he is wrong, forgive. Jesus set the model for us on the cross when He prayed for those who were killing Him, "Father, forgive them, because they do not know what they are doing" (Luke 23:34).

Guidelines to reconcile with those who have offended you:

1. Forgive the offender. Forgiveness is a command, not an option: "Bear with each other and forgive whatever grievances you may have against one another. Forgive as the Lord forgave you" (Colossians 3:13, NIV). "If you don't forgive people, your Father will not forgive your wrongdoing" (Matthew 6:15).

2. You cannot forgive and love in your own strength. The Holy Spirit of Christ in you can enable you to forgive and love. Ask Him to enable you to forgive.

3. Forgiveness is a choice of your will, not the result of a feeling. You must choose to forgive.

4. Begin to pray for God to work in the person's life for his or her good. Continue praying until you can do so with a sincere desire for God to bless the person.

5. Make an investment in the person who wronged you by returning good for evil. Ask God to guide you in this response and in its timing. Ask Him what you can do to meet a need or to show love.

---

1. Claude King, *Come to the Lord's Table* (Nashville: LifeWay Press, 2006). Used by permission.

Telling the Story of Jesus

Before people can benefit from hearing the story of Jesus, they need to understand that they need a Savior. God's Holy Spirit is the One who brings conviction of sin. That is His job. You can pray that He will do that in the lives of those you know who need Christ. God's Word explains that "all have sinned and fall short of the glory of God" (Romans 3:23). God uses sorrow over sin to lead people to repentance: "Godly sorrow produces repentance leading to salvation, not to be regretted" (2 Corinthians 7:10, NKJV).

Another truth people need to understand is that they cannot save themselves. No amount of good works is sufficient to pay their sin debt. "By grace you are saved through faith, and this is not from yourselves; it is God's gift—not from works, so that no one can boast" (Ephesians 2:8-9). Apart from the work of Jesus on the cross, no one can be saved from their own sin. We have no hope without Christ. But the good news is that Jesus suffered and died to satisfy God's requirement for sin's penalty. He offers forgiveness and salvation as free gifts!

According to Scripture, "God's kindness is intended to lead you to repentance" (Romans 2:4). Godly sorrow can cause a person to turn from his sin to Christ, but God's kindness and love demonstrated on the cross can do the job as well. That's why I want you to be prepared to tell the story of Jesus. Jesus paid for our sins when He died on the cross. Then He showed His power over sin and death when God raised Him up from the dead. Just as God raised Jesus from the dead, He can raise us up to live a new life that is free from the penalty and control of sin (Romans 6:4-7).

Telling *your* story is the way you witness to the world. But people also need to know what God has done through Jesus Christ that provides for their salvation. Jesus paid their death penalty on the cross so that they could be forgiven. Learn to tell the story of Jesus to people who need to know Him. Some of the stories you can tell include:

- how God so loved the world that He sent His only Son so that they could be saved from their sin (John 3:16);
- how Jesus lived a life without sin so that He could be the perfect sacrifice for us;
- how Jesus helped people into a right relationship with God; good examples are the Samaritan woman (John 4:4-42), the demon-possessed man (Mark 5:1-20), and the tax collector Zacchaeus (Luke 19:1-10);
- how Jesus was arrested, falsely accused, beaten, abused, and killed on a cruel cross;
- how Jesus rose from the dead and showed Himself to His disciples over a period of 40 days;
- how all these things were prophesied about Him long before the events took place;
- how He ascended into heaven, where He lives now to pray for us.

When you have told the good news about Jesus, explain how the person can receive this free gift of eternal life:

- Receive Him and believe in His name (John 1:12).
- Believe in Him (Acts 10:43).
- Confess (agree with God) that Jesus is Lord—your Master and Ruler.
- Believe God raised Christ from the dead.
- Trust in Him.
- Call on the Lord—ask Him to forgive you and save you (Romans 10:9-13).

Courses to Help You Grow in Discipleship

Ordering Information

Order by calling (800) 458-2772, order online at *www.lifeway.com*, e-mail *orderentry@lifeway.com*, or visit your local LifeWay Christian Store. Ask about the variety of resources, including member books, leader guides, kits, video, DVD, and audio content that might be available.

All Disciplines

• *MasterLife* is a discipleship course from which we drew the Disciple's Cross. It is the course that inspired Dámaris Carbaugh's music to which you've been listening. See page 93 for resources available. (Four 6-session courses)
• Growing Disciples Series. *The Call to Follow Christ* is the first in a series of courses to help you grow spiritually. Check one of the places under "Ordering Information" for available courses. (6 sessions each)

Abide in Christ

• *Experiencing God.* Over five million have studied this course to know and do God's will and to experience Him working in and through them. It helps you grow in your love relationship with Christ and learn to identify when God is speaking to you. (13 sessions)
• *The Mind of Christ* helps you focus on the character and teaching of Christ and become like Him as God shapes you into the image of His Son. (12 sessions)

Live in the Word

• *Step by Step Through the Old Testament* and *Step by Step Through the New Testament* introduce you book by book to the message and meaning of God's Word. (13 sessions each)
• *Living God's Word* helps you learn to study and apply God's Word. (6 sessions)

Pray in Faith

• *Disciple's Prayer Life* is the course by T. W. Hunt that radically impacted my prayer life. It will help you grow deep in a life of prayer and intercession. (13 sessions)

Fellowship with Believers

• *Your Church Experiencing God Together* helps you understand how the body of Christ is to function in carrying out God's purposes. (8 sessions)

Witness to the World

• *Share Jesus Without Fear* helps you share a faithful witness to Christ through everyday conversation. The goal of each witnessing experience is simply to ask five questions and rely on the Holy Spirit to do the convicting and convincing. (4 sessions)
• *Learning to Share My Faith* equips you to use a Roman Road witnessing plan to present the gospel effectively to lost persons, mark key verses in a New Testament, analyze a person's evangelistic potential, cultivate prospects, overcome barriers to witnessing, and follow through after professions of faith. (6 sessions)

Minister to Others

• *Every Christian a Minister* helps you understand biblical truths about ministry and encourages you to find your place in kingdom service. (4 sessions)

Leader Guide

If you have not read the introductory remarks on pages 5–7, do so before continuing.

Jesus gave a final command to His followers: "Go, therefore, and make disciples of all nations, … teaching them to observe everything I have commanded you" (Matthew 28:19-20). As people come to faith in Christ, we have the task of teaching them obedience to all He commanded. That is a huge assignment that we must take seriously. Leading a small-group study of *The Call to Follow Christ* is one way you can obey the final command. Our goal is to help new and growing believers in Jesus Christ develop a balanced, well-rounded spiritual life. We will do that by helping them understand and practice six spiritual disciplines.

Selecting a Leader

Though young believers could study this book together and help one another grow, enlisting a mature believer to lead the group will help the process significantly. The six disciplines we study are the same as those taught in *MasterLife* by Avery T. Willis Jr. Although not required, experience with *MasterLife* would prepare excellent leaders for *The Call to Follow Christ*. Select a leader who has a warm, personal, and faithful walk with Christ. Look for good interpersonal skills and the ability to facilitate small-group learning activities.

Small-Group Study

This resource has been designed for a combination of individual and small-group study. In a small group of other believers, Christians can learn from one another, encourage and strengthen one another,

and minister to one another. The body of Christ can function best as members assume responsibility for helping one another grow in Christlikeness. Encourage participants to study the member book during the week and then join other believers in the small group to process and apply what they have learned. Provide a separate group for every 8 to 12 participants so that everyone will be able to participate actively.

One-to-One Mentoring

If circumstances prevent your studying this in a small-group setting in which you have access to a variety of gifts, you may choose to use it in a one-to-one mentoring process. To do so, study the devotionals each day and meet at least once each week to discuss what you are learning. Use the session plans to get ideas for your personal discussions and prayer time. Talk to each other on the phone in order to pray for and encourage one another.

Enlisting Participants

New believers and those who have not received much help in spiritual growth will benefit most from this introduction to six important spiritual disciplines. As you enlist participants, give members a book before the first session and ask them to study the introduction and week 1 prior to the session. Include other more mature believers in the group so that each subgroup will include someone who will be comfortable praying for the others and who can lead out in discussion.

Your Role as the Leader

You are not required to be a content expert to teach this course. Participants study the content during the week. Your role is to facilitate group discussion, share, and pray to process and apply what participants have learned during the week. Be sensitive to the growth of members and pay special attention to those who may struggle along the way. Don't hesitate to enlist the help of more mature believers in the group to help you nurture the others.

Time and Schedule

This course is designed for seven sessions. The group sessions need to follow the study of the week's daily devotions. Members will need to have books so that they can study the first week's material prior to the first session. Allow at least 60 minutes—preferably 90—for the session. The longer session will provide adequate time for personal sharing, discussion, and prayer for one another.

Optional Introductory Retreat

If you want to jump-start the experience of biblical fellowship *(koinonia)*, conduct a retreat to start the study. Use the content of the first week and the first group session to conduct the retreat. Spend more time getting acquainted. Plan for times of fellowship around meals and recreation. Provide quiet times for individuals to study the individual lessons and come together to process the lessons two or three times during the retreat. Include personal testimonies from those who have been following Christ for a while.

Preparing for the Study

Make prayer a major part of your preparation throughout the course. God will work and guide in answer to prayer, and you will model one of the disciplines in the process. The leadership of the small-group sessions should not require large amounts of time in advance preparation. Take time each week to study the suggestions on the following pages. Use these as options, not as a rigid structure to follow. Allow the needs of your group to dictate the emphasis you give to each topic. Decide which activities and questions to use in your study and determine approximate times for transition between segments. Select activities that are most appropriate for your group's maturity level.

Preparing for Group Sessions

The following suggestions should cover your needs for additional material, resources, and equipment for the sessions.

- *All sessions.* Provide chart paper or a dry-erase board and markers. Bring a CD player for the message music if you intend to use it during the singing/listening segment.
- *Session 1.* Prepare a poster or puzzle of the Disciple's Cross (p. 93) as a visual to be used throughout the study. Make a puzzle, if you like, by cutting a poster into pieces so that you can build the cross one discipline at a time. If you prefer, you can draw the cross live each week. If you have a copy of *MasterLife Leader Kit,* you can use the video presentation of the Disciple's Cross on video 2 rather than drawing it live.
- *Session 3.* Secure an example of some or all of the kinds of Bible study tools listed on pages 94–95 so that members can see the tools and decide which ones they may want to use in their personal Bible study. Research the small-group Bible study options offered by your church and be prepared to answer questions members may have about possible participation (see p. 41).

- *Session 6.* Provide a blank sheet of paper for each member. On page 78 activity 1 lists some tools a person could use to introduce Christ to others. Provide a variety of samples that members can review before or during the session.
- *Session 6.* Go to *www.lifeway.com/discipleship* and download the Spiritual Growth Assessment Tool. Duplicate copies of pages 2–5 for each member in your group. Distribute at the end of session 6 and ask members to complete the personal assessment prior to the final session. Use this information to help members develop an intentional growth plan. Invite members to share their findings as you discuss next steps for growth in discipleship during session 7.
- *Session 7.* So that members will not have to tear the page out of their books, copy the Christian Growth Study Plan form on page 111 and complete the "Church Information" section. Then make a copy for each participant. As they arrive at the final session, ask each member to complete a copy of the form. Sign and date the forms and mail them to the address on the form. For more information go to *www.lifeway.com/cgsp.*

During the Session

Select and arrange the activities and discussion questions based on your group's interest and maturity. Adapt the plans to best meet your group's needs. Here are a few thoughts:

1. *Prayer.* Young believers may not be ready to pray aloud in a group. I've tried to make the prayer activities progressive. Begin by asking for volunteers. Don't call on people to pray unless you know they could do so comfortably. Give permission for people not to pray aloud until they are ready. Seek to increase their prayer participation as the study progresses.
2. *Smaller groups.* Sometimes for sharing I've suggested smaller groupings to increase participation and reduce fear of the large group. The guide will indicate whether to split into pairs or groups of four.
3. *Opening prayer and singing/listening.* If your group is open to singing together, do it. You may want to use familiar praise and worship songs or let them sing along with Dámaris Carbaugh. At times listening to Dámaris sing may be best.
4. *Building relationships.* These activities are more surface, get-acquainted topics that grow deeper as the weeks go by. Adjust the sharing if your group is already well acquainted.
5. *Building the Disciple's Cross.* These activities help participants begin teaching others about the disciplines. Teaching others will help them deepen their understanding.
6. *Responding to learning activities.* Model sharing based on your own responses. Give several people or all an opportunity to share their responses.
7. *Reviewing this week's material.* These activities help you review the facts or key ideas.
8. *Previewing next week.* Use the introductory page to give a quick overview of the upcoming week's study. You could invite volunteers to be prepared in advance to introduce the next discipline.
9. *Praying together.* Use the suggestions on page 96 to encourage praying together as the group matures. Watch for opportunities to pause and pray as a group for needs of specific members of your group.

Session 1 • *Introducing The Call to Follow Christ*

Opening Prayer & Singing/Listening

Building Relationships
Share the following to introduce yourself:
1. Name and information about your immediate family
2. In what city or town did you live most while growing up?
3. Where do you spend most of your waking hours during the week (business or work, home, school, etc.)?
4. What's one interesting fact about you that many people wouldn't know?
5. Why did you decide to participate in this study?

Responding to Learning Activities
1. Page 10, activity 1 and why?
2. Page 18, activity 1 and why?

Interacting with the Scriptures
1. Invite a volunteer to quote Luke 9:23.
2. (p. 15) What truth from Romans 6 about sin's influence in your life is most encouraging to you and why? What are some things you can do to grow in your experience of the reality of Romans 6?
3. What verse or passage of Scripture has been most meaningful or challenging to you this week and why?
4. What significant or meaningful action have you taken because of something God revealed in His Word?
5. Which of the optional readings was most meaningful to you and why?

Responding to God in Prayer
Invite one or two volunteers to respond to God in prayer. Include prayers of thanksgiving for God's call to be a follower of Jesus Christ.

Reviewing Week 1
1. (p. 13) How would you define *disciple* in your own words? What is a disciple of Jesus Christ?
2. (pp. 14–15) If a person wants to follow Christ, what three things must he or she do? Discuss what each means or requires.
3. (pp. 16–17) What are three approaches to knowing, understanding, and applying God's Word in following Christ? Describe each of the ways. Invite volunteers to share their responses to activity 4.
4. (pp. 18–19) As a group and without looking in your books, name and briefly describe each of the six disciplines (one person per discipline, if possible).
5. Review "Tips for Memorizing Scripture" (p. 92). What are some other techniques you have found that help you?

Building the Disciple's Cross
1. Using your poster, puzzle, or a live drawing of the Disciple's Cross, explain each of the six disciplines as an overview for the course. (Note: If you have *MasterLife Leader Kit*, you may choose to show the Disciple's Cross segment on video 2.)
2. How did you respond to activity 2 on page 19?

Previewing Next Week
Use the description and overview on page 21 to preview your study for the coming week.

Praying Together
Pray for the group and ask the Lord to draw each person into an intimate love relationship in which Christ truly abides in each one.

Session 2 • *Abide in Christ*

Opening Prayer & Singing/Listening

Building Relationships
Invite each member to share a brief response to *one* of the following:
1. Describe one close human relationship you have had with a family member or friend.
2. Describe the relationship you have had with your earthly father and how it has affected your relationship with your Heavenly Father.

Building the Disciple's Cross
Using your poster, puzzle, or a live drawing of the Disciple's Cross, focus attention on Abide in Christ in the center circle and invite a volunteer to briefly explain this discipline.

Interacting with the Scriptures
1. Invite volunteers to quote John 15:5.
2. In John 14–15 what is the relationship among our love for Christ, His love for us, and the keeping of His commands?
3. What passage of Scripture has been most meaningful to you this week and why?
4. What significant or meaningful action have you taken because of something God revealed in His Word?
5. Which of the optional readings was most meaningful to you and why?

Responding to God in Prayer
Invite a volunteer or two to respond to God in prayer. Ask the Lord to draw you into close and abiding relationships with Jesus, the true Vine.

Reviewing Week 2
1. (p. 22) What does the word *abide* mean, and how does the parable of the Vine illustrate how we abide in Christ?

2. (p. 22, activity 2) What is the function for each of the following persons in the parable: the Father, Jesus, disciples/followers of Jesus Christ?
3. (p. 24) How was Jesus related to the Father in His words and works?
4. (p. 26) What lessons can we learn from how Jesus spent time with His Father?
5. (pp. 28–29) What spiritual fruit does Jesus expect from the branches?

Responding to Learning Activities
1. Page 23, activity 3 and what do you want your attitude to be, if different?
2. Page 25, activity 2. Discuss the four statements and correct the false one.
3. Page 27, ask volunteers to describe the time they had with the Heavenly Father this week.
4. Page 28, activity 1. Share two high ratings and two lows.

Applying the Truths to Life
1. What are you having to do less of in order to complete *The Call to Follow Christ* lessons?
2. What are some ways God may prune your life and schedule to make you more fruitful? How do your choices improve or hinder the benefits of God's pruning work?
3. What are some ways you can cultivate a more intimate relationship with Jesus?

Previewing Next Week
Use page 33 to preview the study for next week.

Praying Together
Invite volunteers to share requests for their personal relationships with Christ. Close with prayer for these requests.

Opening Prayer & Singing/Listening

Building Relationships

Briefly describe an experience in which you felt great joy and fulfillment or deep hurt or pain. How did you respond, and how was God involved?

Responding to God in Prayer

Invite one or two volunteers to respond to God in prayer. Include prayers for those who may still be wounded and hurting. Praise and thank Him for the good things He has done.

Building the Disciple's Cross

Using your poster, puzzle, or a live drawing of the Disciple's Cross, add the Live in the Word post to the Abide in Christ circle. In pairs ask one person to describe Abide in Christ and the other to describe Live in the Word.

Responding to Learning Activities

1. Page 34, activity 1
2. Page 35, activity 2 and why?
3. Page 37, activity 2
4. Page 37, activity 5
5. Page 43, activities 3–4 (invite volunteers to show their artwork to the group)
6. Page 43, activity 5

Interacting with the Scriptures

1. Invite volunteers to quote Luke 9:23, John 15:5, and James 1:22.
2. In what way has God spoken to you through His Word and urged you to respond in obedience? What was the Scripture, and what did you do to obey?
3. What has God revealed of His will through a Scripture but you chose *not* to obey, and

what were the consequences?
4. What verse or passage of Scripture has been most meaningful or challenging to you this week and why?
5. What significant or meaningful action have you taken because of something God revealed in His Word?
6. Which of the optional readings was most meaningful to you and why?

Reviewing Week 3

1. List ways you can interact with Scripture to get the truths from the page into your mind, heart, and life.
2. (pp. 38–39) What are some valuable reasons for memorizing God's Word?
3. (pp. 40–41, 94–95) What are some ways to study God's Word, and what tools are available to help you do so?

Applying the Truths to Life

1. What reading plans or devotional guides have been meaningful to you as you have read and studied God's Word in the past?
2. (pp. 38–39) What are some of the benefits of memorizing Scripture? How did Jesus use the Scripture?
3. (p. 41) What are the small-group Bible study options available in your church and community? Which one has been most meaningful to you and why?

Previewing Next Week

Use page 45 to preview the study for next week.

Praying Together

Invite volunteers to pray brief, conversational prayers in response to what God is saying through His Word and doing in your lives.

Session 4 • *Pray in Faith*

Opening Prayer & Singing/Listening

Building the Disciple's Cross
Using your poster, puzzle, or a live drawing of the Disciple's Cross, add the Pray in Faith post to complete the vertical bar. In pairs ask members to alternate describing each of the first three disciplines.

Reviewing Week 4
1. (p. 46) How would you define *prayer* in your own words?
2. (p. 47) Without looking, see how many of the "10 Reasons to Pray" your group can name. Then check yourselves.
3. (pp. 48–49) What are four types of responding prayers, and what aspect of God are you responding to in each? Describe or give an example of each.
4. (p. 50) What are some things that keep our prayers from being answered?
5. (p. 55) What are things that hinder prayers of agreement?
6. (pp. 52–53) What are four reasons you can give God to answer your prayer? Explain each and discuss when it would be an appropriate reason to give God in prayer.

Building Relationships
If your group is large, divide into smaller groups of four to six persons each. Share your responses to activities 4 and 5 on page 47 and activity 1 on page 54. As each person shares his or her major prayer request, ask one or two volunteers to pray for that request. Continue until you have prayed for each person.

Responding to Learning Activities
1. Page 51, activity 3

Applying the Truths to Life
1. How can you best prepare yourself to pray with power?
2. Which suggestions did you underline on page 96 as particularly important? Which of these, if any, is different from the way you have typically experienced praying together?

Responding to God in Prayer
Practice praying together, following these suggestions. Focus your prayers on praying for your group and your church—that you will increasingly become a people who are powerful in prayer. Pray for an extended time, and the leader will close the prayer time.

Interacting with the Scriptures
1. Invite volunteers to quote Luke 9:23, John 15:5, James 1:22, and Mark 11:24.
2. What are some requests Jesus made in His prayer in John 17? (p. 50, activity 1)
3. What verse or passage of Scripture has been most meaningful or challenging to you this week and why?
4. What significant or meaningful action have you taken because of something God revealed in His Word?
5. Which of the optional readings was most meaningful to you and why?

Previewing Next Week
Use page 57 to preview the study for next week.

Praying Together
Turn to page 49. Invite everyone to pray brief prayers of praise, worship, and thanksgiving. If needed, use the attributes, biblical words for praise and worship, Scriptures, or examples in your prayers. You may pray more than once.

Session 5 • *Fellowship with Believers*

Opening Prayer & Singing/Listening

Building the Disciple's Cross

Using your poster, puzzle, or a live drawing of the Disciple's Cross, add the Fellowship with Believers bar to the first three disciplines. In pairs ask members to alternate describing each of the four disciplines studied thus far.

Building Relationships

In group of four describe a time in your life when you either needed forgiveness or were called on to forgive another. How did you respond?

Responding to Learning Activities

1. Page 59, activity 3
2. Page 60, activity 2
3. Page 62, activity 1
4. Page 63, activity 3
5. Page 65, activities 3–4
6. Page 67, activities 4–5

Interacting with the Scriptures

1. Invite volunteers to quote the five Scriptures you have memorized up to this date.
2. What verse or passage of Scripture has been most meaningful or challenging to you this week and why?
3. What significant or meaningful action have you taken because of something God revealed in His Word?
4. Which of the optional readings was most meaningful to you and why?

Responding to God in Prayer

Invite one or two volunteers to pray for yourselves and your church, that you will live in unity and harmony with one another.

Reviewing Week 5

1. (p. 59) What are some of the consequences of holding on to bitterness and unforgiveness?
2. (p. 60) How would you define the word *fellowship* in your own words?
3. (p. 61) What four things was the early church devoted to? How does the 21st-century church measure by those standards?
4. (p. 65) What are some things God might want you to lay down because you love your brothers and sisters in Christ?
5. (pp. 64–65) How would you define *love?*
6. (pp. 66–67) What attitudes or character traits contribute to maintaining unity in the body of Christ? Which attitudes and traits would more likely cause division?
7. (p. 67) What are some evidences that a person or a church is proud rather than humble?

Applying the Truths to Life

1. Suppose you were counseling a person filled with bitterness over an offense that took place years ago. Now the offender is dead. What would you say to help him or her?
2. If prejudice in a church existed toward Christians of other skin colors, ethnic backgrounds, national origin, or economic status, what would that tell you about the church? If you had to preach a sermon to that church, what Scriptures would you use?
3. What are some ways Christians demonstrate love in the body of Christ?

Previewing Next Week

Use page 69 to preview the study for next week.

Praying Together

In groups of four ask, How may we pray for you? Then pray for each person's request.

Session 6 • *Witness to the World*

Opening Prayer & Singing/Listening

Building the Disciple's Cross
Distribute blank sheets of paper and ask members to draw the Disciple's Cross, including the circle and the vertical and horizontal bars. In pairs ask members to alternate describing each of the five disciplines studied thus far.

Building Relationships
Briefly tell the story of the demon-possessed man who was set free by Jesus (Mark 5:1-20) and read Jesus' instructions to him in Mark 5:19. In groups of four ask members to tell their own stories of when and how they came into a saving relationship with Jesus Christ and how much the Lord has done for them (p. 77).

Responding to Learning Activities
1. Page 71, activities 2–3
2. Page 78, activity 1

Interacting with the Scriptures
1. Invite volunteers to quote Luke 9:23, John 15:5, James 1:22, Mark 11:24, Hebrews 10:24-25, and Acts 1:8.
2. In 1 Corinthians 9:19-22 why did Paul make himself "a slave to all"?
3. What lessons can we learn from the Samaritan woman at the well about when and how a person can be a witness for Christ?
4. What verse or passage of Scripture has been most meaningful or challenging to you this week and why?
5. What significant or meaningful action have you taken because of something God revealed in His Word?
6. Which of the optional readings was most meaningful to you and why?

Reviewing Week 6
1. (p. 70) What was Jesus' final command, and why do you think He repeated it several times and in different ways?
2. (p. 75) What are some ways you can cultivate relationships with those who need Christ?
3. (p. 79) What do you think it would mean for us to be Christ's witnesses to Jerusalem, Judea, Samaria, and the ends of the earth?

Responding to God in Prayer
Turn to page 73. In groups of four discuss, Who is the person you would most like to see come to faith in Christ (activity 4) and why? Using the suggestions for ways to pray for those yet to believe, pray for the persons you have just described. Pray for one another as you seek to be witnesses to these you love and care about.

Applying the Truths to Life
(pp. 74–75) Summarize the story of a church that showed God's love and mercy. Discuss ways you can help one another minister to and reach out to the persons for whom you have just prayed. How did you respond to activity 2 on page 78? Discuss what you can do to help one another reach out to these who need Christ.

Praying Together
In small groups pray by name for those who need Christ. Ask God to give you boldness to be His witnesses. Ask Him to give you the Holy Spirit's power to bring them to faith in Jesus. Ask Him to guide you in taking some next steps this week.

Previewing Next Week
Use page 81 to preview the study for next week.

Session 7 • Minister to Others

Opening Prayer & Singing/Listening

Arrival Activity
Invite members who have completed this study to fill out the Christian Growth Study Plan form on the following page. (You may duplicate the form with church information completed, if desired.) Collect completed forms, sign and date them, and mail as directed on the form.

Building the Disciple's Cross
Using your poster, puzzle, or a live drawing of the Disciple's Cross, add the ministry arrows. Invite volunteers to name each of the ministries around the cross that make up the Minister to Others discipline. In pairs ask members to alternate describing each of the six disciplines.

Building Relationships
Describe a time when you or your immediate family had a special need and received ministry from one or more members in the body of Christ. Or describe a time when you became aware of a need and God worked through you to meet that need in love.

Responding to Learning Activities
1. Page 83, activity 4
2. Page 85, prayer activities. What, if anything, do you sense God wants you to do in ministry to others?
3. Pages 88–89, activities 1–2
4. Pages 90–91, activities 3–6

Interacting with the Scriptures
1. Invite volunteers to quote Luke 9:23, John 15:5, James 1:22, Mark 11:24, Hebrews 10:24-25, Acts 1:8, and Galatians 5:13.
2. Read Ephesians 4:11-13. Review responses to activity 1 on page 84. Discuss ways God might use members of the body in works of service to build up the body of Christ.
3. (p. 86) What do we learn from Matthew 25:31-46 about how Jesus looks on lowly service to needy people around us? If Jesus showed up at your church today to make this judgment, how do you think He would respond to most of your members?
4. What verse or passage of Scripture has been most meaningful or challenging to you this week and why?

Responding to God in Prayer
Invite one or two volunteers to respond to God in prayer. Ask the Lord to enable you to be faithful servants to people in need.

Reviewing Week 7
1. (p. 82) What are some ways humans typically claim greatness or influence? (See activity 2.) What did Jesus describe as the way to greatness in His kingdom? How did He model this kind of service?
2. (p. 85) What are five types of ministry described by the Disciple's Cross? Discuss ways each of those ministries might be undertaken in your church and community.
3. (pp. 90, 100) Discuss the next steps you sense God wants you to take in your personal growth in discipleship. Consider options already planned by your church.

Praying Together
As time permits (either all together or in small groups), ask each person, How may we pray for your growth in discipleship? Then have one or two members pray for each person. Close with a prayer of thanksgiving for what God has done.

Two Ways to Earn Credit
for Studying LifeWay Christian Resources Material

CHRISTIAN GROWTH STUDY PLAN

CONTACT INFORMATION:
Christian Growth Study Plan
One LifeWay Plaza, MSN 117
Nashville, TN 37234
CGSP info line 1-800-968-5519
www.lifeway.com/CGSP
To order resources 1-800-458-2772

Christian Growth Study Plan resources are available for course credit for personal growth and church leadership training.

Courses are designed as plans for personal spiritual growth and for training current and future church leaders. To receive credit, complete the book, material, or activity. Respond to the learning activities or attend group sessions, when applicable, and show your work to your pastor, staff member, or church leader. Then go to *www.lifeway.com/CGSP*, or call the toll-free number for instructions for receiving credit and your certificate of completion.

For information about studies in the Christian Growth Study Plan, refer to the current catalog online at the CGSP Web address. This program and certificate are free LifeWay services to you.

Need a CEU?

CONTACT INFORMATION:
CEU Coordinator
One LifeWay Plaza, MSN 150
Nashville, TN 37234
Info line 1-800-968-5519
www.lifeway.com/CEU

Receive Continuing Education Units (CEUs) when you complete group Bible studies by your favorite LifeWay authors.

Some studies are approved by the Association of Christian Schools International (ACSI) for CEU credits. Do you need to renew your Christian school teaching certificate? Gather a group of teachers or neighbors and complete one of the approved studies. Then go to *www.lifeway.com/CEU* to submit a request form or to find a list of ACSI-approved LifeWay studies and conferences. Book studies must be completed in a group setting. Online courses approved for ACSI credit are also noted on the course list. The administrative cost of each CEU certificate is only $10 per course.